mission shaped intro

What is a fresh expression of church?

A **fresh expression** is a form of church for our changing culture, established primarily for the benefit of people who are not yet members of any church.

It will come into being through principles of listening, service, incarnational mission and making disciples.

It will have the potential to become a mature expression of church shaped by the gospel and the enduring marks of the church and for its cultural context.

Fresh expressions of church:

- serve those outside church;
- listen to people and enter their culture;
- make discipleship a priority;
- form church.

The Fresh Expressions organisation exists to encourage and resource these new ways of being church, working with Christians from a broad range of denominations and traditions. The movement has resulted in thousands of new congregations being formed alongside more traditional churches.

Contents

Introduction

The overall aim of *mission shaped intro* is to give people a fresh vision of mission and how we might reshape the church in the light of our ever-changing culture.

About the course

mission shaped intro is designed to help participants reflect upon changes in culture and society and the responses needed to engage in mission in meaningful and relevant ways. It won't equip people to go out and start fresh expressions, but it will challenge people's thinking and help to change their mindset.

If you are looking for a course which explores how to start and sustain a fresh expression of church, visit the website to find out about the *mission shaped ministry* course, a one-year, part-time course which trains participants for ministry in fresh expressions of church.

Don't forget to register your course - details over the page.

Course website, for updates to the notes, additional materials, course fliers, registration and feedback and other information.
bit.ly/msicourse

mission shaped intro web page
freshexpressions.org.uk/missionshapedintro

mission shaped ministry web page
freshexpressions.org.uk/missionshapedministry

One of the most important resources for those in fresh expressions of church is the Guide, an online learning resource. Pages helpful for each session are highlighted throughout these notes. freshexpressions.org.uk/guide

☑ Session checklist
(refer to list at start of each session)

✋ Title, paragraph or list also included in workbook (may be abridged)

✐ Aim of the session
(also included in workbook)

▭ Outline and timings
(also included in workbook)

👥 Group exercise

◉ Video clip

💬 Presentation

🙏 Worship and prayer

📚 Recommended reading

🖱 Related websites

Notes for course facilitators

This material is not designed to be followed slavishly; the timings are simply a guide and not something to be treated rigidly. Please make the material your own, editing and introducing local examples where possible.

Venue

msi was designed for large groups, however it also works with smaller gatherings such as cell or home groups. For larger groups the best format is café-style, with people sitting around tables in a reasonably-sized room. The key is providing a warm and friendly learning atmosphere that will create fellowship. It is ideal if drinks are available before and throughout each session. A bowl of sweets or fruit on each table also adds to the atmosphere. This course can provide an opportunity for ecumenical partnerships in a local area as the material is relevant to a wide audience.

Preparation

The first time you use this course you will need to allow three to four hours of preparation for every hour of delivery to familiarise yourself with the material and to add your own local flavour. The key is to get the information across in a fun and informative way that will encourage and challenge participants rather than speak down to them. A key value of fresh expressions is experimentation and that means that this course will not provide all the answers, but start conversations that include the whole church.

Participants' workbooks are available from freshexpressions.org.uk/shop. Decide whether these are appropriate to your group and, if so, purchase enough for each participant. Discounts are available for bulk orders.

An A5 flier to help publicise the course can be found on the course DVD, as can a PowerPoint publicity slide and an article for newsletters, magazines or newspapers.

Course facilitation

When presenting this course to a large group (20+) the most effective way is to use two facilitators per session. This has a two-fold advantage: the first is that the change of facilitator during the session provides a break of voice and style which helps the learning process and the second is that it increases the number of experienced people when you wish to present the course to other groups. For smaller groups such as cells and home groups you may wish to shorten each session (suggestion of 90 minutes) or may wish to run it over more sessions.

It is important with large courses to divide participants into groups of four to six to allow good interaction with group work and discussions. If the course is being run ecumenically it helps if groups can be mixed up from different churches and groups. This adds to the learning experience by hearing from others who may have different perspectives of church.

Equipment

msi has been designed to be delivered with a full multimedia setup. For larger venues you will need a data projector and screen, laptop, DVD player, CD player and sound system to show the PowerPoint presentations and play the DVD/music clips. In smaller groups you may be able to use a DVD player, TV and CD player but you will still need to project, print off or otherwise make sure that all participants can see the PowerPoint presentations during the sessions.

Course DVD

The course DVD contains all of the clips prepared specifically for the course, which will play on a standard DVD player or through a DVD player on a computer. Additionally, the six PowerPoint presentations and additional materials can be accessed by navigating to the 'presentations' folder of the DVD using your computer's file browser - you should copy these presentations to your computer and run them from there to allow you to play the DVD clips at the same time.

You will need to obtain the well-known films and TV series recommended. We also recommend two film clips from sermonspice.com which you will need to purchase and download if you want to use them. When adapting the materials, don't be tempted to drop the film clips - they provide light and shade and are an opportunity to re-engage those who may have drifted off!

Copyright and sources

Please ensure that the appropriate copyright licences have been obtained for the delivery of the course, for example any song words you put into the presentations (ccli.co.uk). You will also need to obtain copyright clearance, where relevant, for any material that you add in to the course. You need to use film clips from legally bought or hired DVDs rather than downloaded or copied clips. Short film clips may be used for educational purposes under the copyright act.

Course registration and evaluation

Please register your course online at missionshapedministry.org/register.

Following the course, we would be grateful if you could ask each participant to complete an evaluation form (photocopy p128 or download from the course website). Please collate the responses and return your collated answers to us at missionshapedministry.org/evaluate. Your feedback is vital in continuing to assess and improve the materials.

1. rediscovering mission - what that means for the church

Introduction

Aim

To explore the mission of God as the foundation for any expression of church.

Outline and timings

These notes are written as a script which you can use 'as is' or adapt to your own needs and experiences. Text in this type is notes for the leader, not to be read out.

The material is designed for a two hour session with the times given in the 120min column to the right. To reduce to a 90 minute session we suggest using the timings in the 90min column, or adapting the material yourself to suit the emphasis of your group.

Rediscovering mission		120min	90min
Section one: welcome, introductions and worship		**20min**	**20min**
Welcome	💬	5min	5min
Group introductions	👥	10min	10min
Worship and prayer	🙏	5min	5min
Section two: introducing *Mission-shaped Church*		**5min**	**5min**
About the report	💬	5min	5min
Section three: stories of fresh expressions		**30min**	**20min**
Stories of fresh expressions	💿	10min	10min
Your response - small group discussion	👥	15min	8min
Your response - plenary discussion	👥	5min	2min
Section four: our changing world		**25min**	**15min**
Film clip	💿	3min	3min
Changes in society	💬	22min	12min
Section five: worship		**10min**	**10min**
Pause for praise	🙏	10min	10min
Section six: what would a mission-shaped church look like?		**30min**	**20min**
Mission is...	💬+👥	10min	5min
Marks of mission	💬	10min	5min
Your church mission-shaped	💬+👥	5min	5min
Closing prayer and worship	🙏	5min	5min

Session checklist

Media

Equipment to show clips - laptop, projector, DVD player, TV as required.

Mission Impossible theme (download from iTunes, Amazon or elsewhere).

Mr Bean goes to Church clip, if you are going to use it, or a prepared story of your own if required.

From the course DVD:

* Stories of church [9.14]
  (the first five sections of chapter 1 of *expressions: the dvd - 1*)

* What is a fresh expression of church? [0.40]

Sister Act or *The Simpsons: 'Heaven and Hell'* clip.

Any song words required.

Other materials

Paper and pens.

Sweets and stones for the multi-sensory prayer if required.

Pipe-cleaners - one per person.

If required for the closing prayer and worship, one of:

* paper feet;

* paper, pens and scissors

* paint, large roll of paper, water/towels for rinsing feet.

The course workbooks, one for each participant.

Section one: welcome, introductions and worship

Welcome   5min 💬

Introduce yourself and your fellow presenters:

- who you are, where you are from, what you do.

Play Mission Impossible? music. Give an overview of the course, plus notices and fire exits etc.

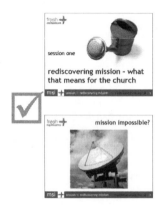

- The aim over the next six sessions is to rediscover mission and to re-examine church.

- This is a whistle-stop tour of current missional thinking for the 21st century - not an in depth traditional Bible study - lots to think about.

- All of us are learning. We don't know everything, so want to hear and learn from you.

- This course is about 'mindset change'. It's about 'why' we need to change as the church, as well sharing lots of stories from around the country that will show us what the 'how' looks like for some people.

- There's another course called *mission shaped ministry* which is more about the 'how' and is geared towards a 'tooling up' process -the next stage after this course.

- Make yourself at home: get drinks at any point in the session as you wish.

- In your workbooks there is space to write your own thoughts and questions. Try journalling what God might be saying to you as you go. How do you feel about what's being said? What questions does it raise?

- We'll give you book and resources recommendations each session to support your learning on this subject, for you to use as you wish.

- We would like to encourage you to talk to others here. You'll learn as much from each other as you will from us. Talk about what God is doing in your area and community; find out the challenges and joys that others are facing.

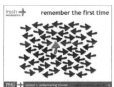

Group introductions

10min 👪

It may help to ring a bell or have another way of signalling two minutes each time.

Talking to others is what we're going to do now. Find one person that you haven't spoken to before, and talk to them about your first experiences of church. That could have been as a child, a teenager or an adult. You'll need to stand up and move around. It's a bit like speed dating! You've got two minutes.

Next, find someone else you haven't spoken to before and talk to them about your best experience of church. What was it and why was it so special? You've got two minutes.

On to another new person. This time tell him or her about your worst experience of church. What was it and why was it so bad? Your two minutes starts now.

Invite people to take their seats.

Having thought about ourselves, let's think of how others may feel.

Either show Mr Bean goes to church, share Jeff's story below or tell a story of your own. At the end make the point that for non-Christians, church of whatever style or denomination can be a strange place full of strange people doing strange things.

Jeff Reynolds' Story

I was 22 years old before I entered church for the first time. A good friend of mine since I was 16 went to church and he got into a regular pattern of asking me to come with him. I was from a total non-church background and it just seemed a pointless thing to do, so I kept saying 'no' to him.

Eventually I made a pact with him that if I went to church just once, he would promise never to ask me again. That would enable me to stop finding creative ways of saying 'no' to a good friend. The great day came and the service began at 6.30pm. I said to my friend that I would get there at 6.29 and sneak in at the back. My first major error was to then completely forget the starting time. Come the said day I had convinced myself that I needed to be there at 5.59 for a 6pm start. This I duly did and found myself wandering into a nearly empty church.

Now I need to say that I'm 6ft 2in tall and it was summer time so I was in my t-shirt, shaven-headed with the swagger of a young twenty-something who did a bit of boxing. There was a lady sitting on the back row, she took one look at me and immediately picked up her handbag and held it tightly. Obviously, I looked an undesirable and some kind of potential thief - welcome to Church! The person on the door had given me two hymn books, a Bible, notice sheet and song sheet because apparently one song wasn't in any of the books and we would be singing it in the service. Very bewildering for a totally non-churched person.

The Church filled up and the service began with a man appearing at the front from a hole in the wall. He was obviously in a rush as he had his shirt on back to front! We then sang a series of songs I didn't know and which were basically impossible to sing with archaic lyrics and bizarre tunes. We sat down and the man at the front led us in prayer. It was at this point that I nearly put my hand up and asked him what prayer was, because I didn't know, but everybody else seemed to know and they all crouched forward like they were preparing for a scrummage but they had their eyes shut.

Next we had a reading from the book of Obadiah. By the time I'd found it (with the help of the index) it had finished. The man at the front, who was by now sweating profusely, spoke at us for about 20 minutes. It was utter drivel with very forced humour and I realised that it was 20 minutes of my life that I would never get back. To cap it all, they had the sheer cheek to ask for money for this 'worship experience!' I was tempted to take a fiver out rather than put 10p in as the plate passed by. I couldn't get out fast enough and won't tell you my response to my friend who said to me after the service, 'did you enjoy that?' Perhaps the most bizarre and baffling part of this story is that I went back the next week and am now the Superintendent of the Stafford Methodist Circuit.

Worship and prayer   5min 🗨

All of us bring our own experiences of and feelings about church to this course. Let's offer them to God now in worship and prayer.

Prepare your own short offering of worship and prayer or select from:

1. Multi-sensory prayer

Invite participants to savour a sweet and as they do so quietly thank God for the times when church has been a particular blessing or joy. Then invite people to place a stone in the centre of their table or room and as they do so quietly offer a prayer of lament for the times when church has been a burden or a painful place to be. Finally invite people to picture someone new in their church. How are they being welcomed, does church appear strange or warm to them? Can they join in or are they confused? As they picture the newcomer ask them to pray quietly for the gifts of welcome and hospitality. Then offer a short prayer drawing the reflections together.

2. Song and prayer

Choose a worship song to sing together. You'll need to put the words on the PowerPoint presentation in advance. Suggestions are to the left.

Let's say this prayer together:

> Almighty God, by your grace you have given us a new life in Jesus Christ, and by your Spirit you have called us to proclaim his name throughout the nations.
>
> Awaken in us such a love for you and for your world that we may boldly proclaim Jesus Christ by word and deed, so that all people may come to know him as Saviour and follow him as Lord, to the glory of your name.
>
> Amen.

♫ Edwin Hatch
Breathe on me Breath of God
Traditional

Nathan Fellingham
Awake, Awake O Zion
Kingsway's Thankyou Music, 1999

fresh expressions — prayer

Almighty God, by your grace you have given us a new life in Jesus Christ, and by your Spirit you have called us to proclaim his name throughout the nations.

fresh expressions — prayer

Awaken in us such a love for you and for your world that we may boldly proclaim Jesus Christ by word and deed, so that all people may come to know him as Saviour and follow him as Lord, to the glory of your name.

Amen

Section two: introducing *Mission-shaped Church*

About the report   5min 💬

Despite all the press reports of falling numbers, there are encouraging signs that a springtime season is beginning in the life of the church, with new growth springing up everywhere.

Mission-shaped Church was published in January 2004. It is the Church of England's bestselling report ever, looked at by every other denomination. Reprinted twice, over 30,000 now sold.

The report coined the phrase 'fresh expression of church' and encouraged support and finance for new ways of being church. The report did not invent fresh expressions - they have been forming since the day of Pentecost! Rather it named something that was going on and gave birth to a new Fresh Expressions movement that has encouraged and nurtured the proliferation of new forms of church that we see today. This new growth is not confined to the UK. There are now fresh expressions movements in many countries and this course, *msi*, has been downloaded on every continent on earth!

Between 2004 and 2012, 2,000 fresh expressions of church were formed in the British Methodist Church and the Church of England, plus more in The Salvation Army, URC, Congregational Federation, Ground Level Network, Church of Scotland and other partner streams and denominations.

In this course we'll be looking at the content and implications of the *Mission-shaped Church* report that has been so influential in the various fresh expressions movements. Here I will introduce some key phrases.

First, a definition:

> A fresh expression is a form of church for our changing culture established primarily for the benefit of people who are not yet members of any church.

Rowan Williams, Archbishop of Canterbury from 2002-12, coined the phrase a 'mixed economy' church, with new ways of being church co-existing alongside our inherited parishes and other traditional forms of church.

We need to learn to be a both/and church:

- **both** treasuring what we have inherited in the church
- **and** valuing and developing the newer forms

It doesn't mean stopping meeting on Sunday mornings, nor does it mean wearing rollerblades to worship! Traditional forms of church are still working well for about 40% of our population, mainly older than younger.

Every church needs to understand its fundamental calling to be a mission-shaped church - to be serving, welcoming, learning, worshipping, discipling, transforming communities. This is not about fresh expressions being about mission and other churches ignoring mission.

Mission-shaped Church was well received by leaders and churchgoers alike. The British Methodist Church, as part of the 'Our Calling' process, passed a resolution at Conference in 2004 affirming fresh expressions as one of its five priority areas.

At a local level Christians of all denominations are joining in this new move of mission.

Section three: stories of fresh expressions

Stories of fresh expressions   10min

There are now hundreds of stories of fresh expressions from a whole range of contexts. Many of these are on the DVDs produced by Fresh Expressions. Even more are available on our website including updates on many of the DVD stories. We're going to see some of those stories now.

Show Stories of church from the course DVD, the start of chapter 1 from expressions: the dvd - 1 [9.14].

*   Taste and See Coffee Shop - Kidsgrove;
*   The Bridge - Hinckley;
*   Legacy XS Skatepark (youth) - Benfleet, Essex;
*   Sanctuary (Asian culture) - Birmingham;
*   Messy Church (all age/families) - Portsmouth.

 Fresh Expressions shop
freshexpressions.org.uk/shop

Fresh Expressions stories and updates
freshexpressions.org.uk/stories

It is important to realise that fresh expressions of church are intended to be precisely that: fresh expressions of *church*, not just renewed worship, imaginative mission or creative youth work. These are all very good and *msi* may inspire you to develop some or all of them, which would be wonderful. But as this clip explains, fresh expression of church are new churches, for new people, in new places - so we need to be careful how we define things.

Show What is a fresh expression of church? from the course DVD [0.40].

Your response   20min (10min)

As this is the first time the group has met, we suggest discussing first in groups of three or four, then inviting feedback. This gives more people opportunity to speak in a less intimidating context.

Invite people to get themselves a drink (omit in a 90min session) and talk in small groups, sharing their responses to the clip.

Section four: our changing world

After 15min (8min in a 90min session), invite each group to summarise their discussion to the larger group. Draw out why people think change is needed within the church and what their questions and reservations are (if any). It's worth quietly noting these so that you can make sure they are addressed through the course.

Film clip   3min ☺

You'll have seen from the video that setting up a fresh expression of church is not about doing youth work! It's about doing church in a way that connects with our friends and the networks that we're involved in. Here's a reminder of why that's necessary, if we need one.

 Play a film clip to suit your audience. You may wish to amend the PowerPoint. Our suggestions are:

* Sister Act: a dead church with empty pews, awful choir and despairing priest (chapter 10, 0:29:24 to 0:31:20, end on long shot down the church);

* The Simpsons: Homer and the children's reluctance to go to church/delight at getting home (From 'In Marge We Trust' on the 'Heaven and Hell' DVD, 0:01:30 - after Itchy and Scratchy to 0:03:40 - Revd Lovejoy: 'I wasn't expecting that').

 ## Changes in society   22min (12min) ☻

We need to respond to the fact that society is always changing, with the pace of change increasing in recent years. In twos or threes, list some of the changes in society that have an impact on the way that we do church, or the assumptions we make about church.

Allow a couple of minutes of discussion.

These are some of the changes in society that *Mission-shaped Church* identified as having a significant impact:

1. Changing Sundays

For a good many people, Sunday is a day of work, or a day for sport, particularly for children. It's an essential time with their families and increasingly a day for contact time between separated or divorced parents and their children. People will be reluctant to sacrifice this precious time for church and will need opportunities for worship and community on other days. This is not a recent change. Rightly or wrongly, Sunday trading was made legal in the UK as long ago as 1994 and the first football league match was played on a Sunday in 1974 (Milwall beat Fulham 1-0 if you really need to know). But still, most Sunday service times are set by when the cows have been milked.

The needs is for church at different times.

2. Changing relationships

The way we relate to others has changed. In general, people today know their neighbours less well, travel more, and live away from parents and extended family. Relationships tend to be formed by networks or leisure activities, some of those happening online rather than face to face. As Christians we need to learn how to relate to people in these new networks not just in our geographical locality.

This will lead to church for different networks.

3. Changing cultures

In the past, there was one recognisable culture shared by most of our society across a generation or two. Today there are many different groups

and subcultures within society, and the church is no longer central to this changing pattern of culture. For example we now have multiple TV channels with smaller and smaller audiences. Yet God calls us to carry the good news to all these different people groups.

This will lead to church in different cultures.

4. Less knowledge of faith

Today people know less and less about Christianity. Imagine how strange you would feel if you went into a betting shop for the first time! It's important that we begin to understand how strange the church is for many people.

This will lead to church for beginners.

5. Deep spiritual hunger

Today, society is more open to spiritual questions and, sadly, people are not banging down our church doors looking for answers. They just don't connect spirituality with the church. We need to find new ways of engaging with the spiritually hungry in their worlds, instead of expecting them to come to ours.

This will lead to church for explorers.

If there is time, invite people to add other changes from their groups. You won't be able to discuss them in depth but acknowledge that they exist and will also have an impact on the way we do church.

As we look at the changes around us and the decline in the numbers of people attending traditional church, it is easy to become anxious or afraid, to blame ourselves or others. Instead, we need to be rooted in God. What we do as a church is rooted in what we believe, and is shaped by the Gospel.

It's tempting to start with the church, as we did in our conversations at the beginning - to try to increase what excites us, to tackle what frustrates us or to copy what we see others doing. But the church needs to be where we end up, not where we begin. We need to start with God - who God is and what God is like.

Three words ending in 'ology' that we're going to consider are:

Theology - missiology - ecclesiology

Our theology affects our missiology which determines our ecclesiology.

Or in English:

• our understanding of God the Father, Son and Holy Spirit must unpack itself,

• through our understanding of mission,

• which then shapes the church,

not the other way round.

If God is creative, holy, just and loving for example then the mission we share and the churches that grow out of that mission should be infused with these characteristics.

What should mission be like? What should our churches be like? Ask what God is like and you are well on the way to the answers.

Developing fresh expressions of church is not some clever strategy to manage ourselves out of decline, as if we could do that. It is a response in our present culture to the Gospel of Jesus Christ.

Going back to our definition of a fresh expression of church, here is the definition in full as offered by the Fresh Expressions initiative:

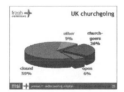

A fresh expression is a form of church for our changing culture established primarily for the benefit of people who are not yet members of any church. It will come into being through principles of listening, service, incarnational mission and making disciples.

These are all principles that we can see in the life of Jesus and the model that he gave us for engaging with the world.

It will have the potential to become a mature expression of church, shaped by the Gospel and the enduring historic marks of the church within and for its cultural context.

There's an expectation of growth and change within fresh expressions of church. A fresh expression may start in one form and develop into another, but we must let them start.

In 2004, *Mission-shaped Church* presented statistics based on research by Philip Richter and Leslie Francis which suggested that roughly 40% of people in Britain were in reach of the traditional church: in round figures, 10% came to church regularly (at least once a month), 10% came a bit, 20% used to come and might have been open to coming back.

The larger proportion, 60%, was made up of:

- 20% who used to come and were not open to returning;
- 40% who had never been part of the church (a very few of whom were open to coming).

Subsequent research published by Tearfund in 2007 (which is soon to be repeated) showed that the proportion of people who were not open to coming to church had continued to grow and stood at 59%, compared to 26% who had some contact with church and just 6% who didn't come but would consider it. The missional challenge is great and growing.

Section five: worship

Pause for praise   10min

Either prepare your own material here or use this exercise to illustrate and reflect on some truth.

Give each person a pipe cleaner and get them to put it on the floor for now. Stand in a circle facing inwards, not touching one another.

For many this is an illustration of church, together but not connected. There's limited trust and intimacy.

Invite people to join hands.

Church needs to be a place of growing trust, love, intimacy, and connectedness.

It needs to be a connected group with pastoral caring for and ministry to each other.

But all we are offering outsiders is our backs, not our eyes or hands.

Invite people to face outward, and join hands again.

We've changed direction, not inward but outward, a change of focus.

Imagine now you are standing on a high point overlooking your neighbourhood.

What do you see, sense, discern, out there?

1 John 1.1 talks about the tangible work of God - what we have heard, seen, looked at and touched. Where is the wind of God blowing in your village/town/city?

Our task is to discover what God is doing and join in or learn from it. It may be in the church or it may be outside the church... in the wider kingdom of God. During the first 40 days of Jesus' ministry, he was tempted by the

kingdom of this world (Matthew 4.9). During his last 40 days, he spoke about the kingdom of God (Acts 1.3). There is a battle of kingdoms in our world.

The initial inward position is more pastorally-orientated. Our outward position is mission-focused.

The church needs to do both but we must recognize that, for most of us, what comes naturally is to be pastoral; we need to take up the challenge to be missional.

Invite people to take their seats and to make a cross out of their pipe cleaner.

The cross represents some of our believing. As you make your cross, I want you to share with the person next to you, something you have seen, sensed or heard that's happening in the church or kingdom of God in this place. Give thanks to God for it.

Now please put your crosses in the centre of the circle, even if unfinished, so that they are all touching.

The touching illustrates the truth about belonging.

The unfinished cross is about beliefs, believing still being formed or discovered.

The crosses are in the centre, a reminder that Jesus needs to be at the centre of our lives and our church. We need to keep Jesus at the centre; he is the reference point, the magnetic north.

If you have time you could sing (suggestion to the left). You will need to create a slide with the words for the song if you choose to use it.

 Michael Frye **Jesus be the** Song **Centre** Vineyard

Section six: what would a mission-shaped church look like?

Mission is...   10min (5min) 💬 👥

We're talking about the need to be mission-shaped. There's so much that could be said about mission. Whole books have been written about it. People have come up with rich and complex definitions of what mission is. But this is a helpful working definition of what mission is:

> Mission is seeing what God is doing and joining in.

Our calling is to be involved in the missio dei - the work of God in the world. But what will that look like? What should we be doing? Think about the things God is doing in this world. What does that mean that we should be engaging in as we participate in his work in the world?

In groups of three or four, create the three priorities you think God wants the church (us) to engage with.

Hand out paper and pens for people to write on. After five minutes, call the group together and get their feedback. Collate the results on the flip chart, creating the group's top five priorities.

Marks of mission   10min (5min) 💬

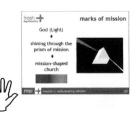

The word 'mission' can be problematic. It is used in many different contexts and can mean many different things. Businesses, charities, agencies can each have 'a mission' and a mission statement to prove it!

The word mission has Latin roots - missio - meaning 'to be sent'.

Christians can disagree over what they are sent to do. In using the word mission, some focus on evangelism, others on serving in the community, others on political action and yet others on loving service. This is the nub of the problem, that mission can mean many different things to many people often resulting in confusion, crossed wires and wasted energy.

The best way through this is to accept the breadth of meaning that is given to the word and to see it simply as a 'range' of different activities that express the light and love of God whose mission it actually is.

Across the denominations this range is sometimes given headings or 'marks of mission'. Visually, mission might be represented as a spectrum: the one presented here is based on the five marks of mission endorsed by the Lambeth Conference 1988 and Forum of Churches Together in England 1997.

Light is composed of different colours (wavelengths actually), a fact discovered by Isaac Newton. These can be seen as white light passing through a prism. Here is a way for the spectrum colours to represent the range of meanings contained within the word 'mission'.

God shines his light through the prism of mission producing these colours:

Red	A 'loud' colour, heralding	Proclaim the Good News of the Kingdom.
Orange Yellow	Colours of spring, new life, new start	To teach, baptise and nurture new believers.
Green	Pastoral, earth, association of the colour with environmental responsibility	To strive to safeguard the integrity of creation and sustain and renew the life of the earth.
Blue	Colour of peace, wholeness and healing	To respond to human need by loving service.
Indigo Violet	Purple, colours of authority, sovereignty, power	To seek to transform unjust structures of society.

The light of God shining through the prism of mission forms mission-shaped church, revealing the one who said 'I am the light of the world'.

Compare and contrast these with the list the group has created. Invite comments and questions.

Your church mission-shaped

5min 💬 👥

Over the six sessions that we will be meeting, we're going to explore how this thinking will impact our own churches, both existing churches and fresh expressions. I want to encourage you to continue reflecting on that between sessions and maybe talk to others in your church about it. But as you've gone through this session, you may already have thought about how your church might need to change if it were to become more mission-shaped. Let's have a minute of quiet to give us a chance to reflect, and then I'm going to invite each of you in turn to say how your church might become more mission-shaped or if you need to consider a fresh expression of church.

Allow a moment of quiet, then invite someone to start the round. People can pass if they want to.

Closing prayer and worship

5min 🗨️

Invite people to hold these thoughts of their own churches in their hearts and minds as you say this prayer together.

Jesus, you invite us to follow you.
Walking in your footsteps will take us to new places,
will introduce us to new people,
will sometimes make us uncomfortable,
will lead us to life in all its fullness.

Help us Lord
to follow where you lead
to join in with what you are already doing in our world
to change to become more like you
In Jesus' name
Amen.

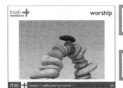

You may like to sing a closing song of worship before or after the prayer. Remember to add the words to the PowerPoint presentation.

If you want to be more creative, before you say the prayer together you could get participants to create a pathway of footsteps by:

- using some paper feet that you cut out earlier;
- getting the group to cut out paper feet for themselves;
- inviting people to step into paint and then onto on a large roll of paper to each leave a trail of footsteps.

Finish

Thank people for coming, point out the book recommendations in the workbook and confirm the arrangements for the next session.

 What Christian principles lie behind fresh expressions?
freshexpressions.org.uk/guide/about/principles

2. changing world, changing church

Introduction

Aim

To explore how the church might respond to a world of change and uncertainty.

Outline and timings

These notes are written as a script which you can use 'as is' or adapt to your own needs and experiences. Text in this type is notes for the leader, not to be read out.

The material is designed for a two hour session with the times given in the 120min column to the right. To reduce to a 90 minute session we suggest using the timings in the 90min column, or adapting the material yourself to suit the emphasis of your group.

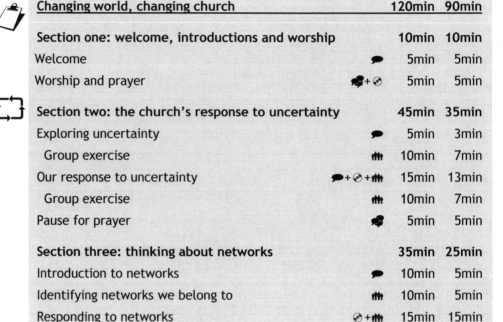

Changing world, changing church		120min	90min
Section one: welcome, introductions and worship		**10min**	**10min**
Welcome	🗨	5min	5min
Worship and prayer	🗨+⊘	5min	5min
Section two: the church's response to uncertainty		**45min**	**35min**
Exploring uncertainty	🗨	5min	3min
Group exercise	👥	10min	7min
Our response to uncertainty	🗨+⊘+👥	15min	13min
Group exercise	👥	10min	7min
Pause for prayer	🗨	5min	5min
Section three: thinking about networks		**35min**	**25min**
Introduction to networks	🗨	10min	5min
Identifying networks we belong to	👥	10min	5min
Responding to networks	⊘+👥	15min	15min
Section four: more about mission		**30min**	**20min**
A new way of thinking about mission	🗨+⊘	5min	5min
Church for my friend	👥	20min	10min
Closing prayer and worship	🗨	5min	5min

Session checklist

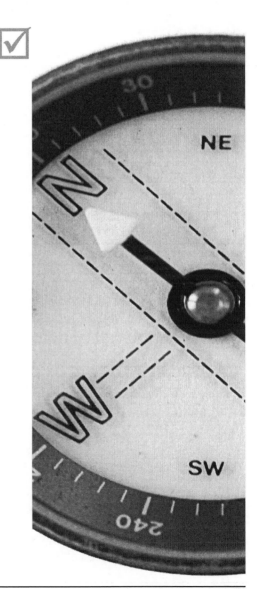

Media

Equipment to show clips - laptop, projector, DVD player, TV as required.

A clip from the week's news, if required.

From the course DVD, one of:

- Cable Street [5.42]
  chapter 14 from *expressions: the dvd - 1*
- The Beacon [8.21]
  chapter 20 from *expressions: making a difference*

Images of local crosses and an appropriate piece of music, if required.

From the course DVD, one of:

- Tubestation [7.12]
  chapter 26 from *expressions: making a difference*
- Riverforce [5.16]
  first part of chapter 1 from *expressions: the dvd - 2*
- Harvest New Anglican Church [7.18]
  chapter 10 from *expressions: making a difference*

From the course DVD:

- Stop starting with the Church [1.57]
  a short film by Peter Dominey and Kezia M'Clelland of
  churchfromscratch.org

Any song words required.

Other materials

Sheets of flipchart paper and pens, or whiteboard and markers.

Section one: welcome, introductions and worship

Welcome   5min

Remind participants who the presenters are, where you are from, what you do.

In the last session we looked at:

- *Mission-shaped Church* report;
- fresh expressions of church and a mixed economy church;
- changes in our society mean changes are needed in the way we do church;
- our understanding of God shapes our understanding of mission which impacts how we do church;
- mission is seeing what God is doing in the world and joining in;
- marks of mission and a mission spectrum.

In this session we will look at the implications of increasing uncertainty in the world, and a move towards relationships being formed through networks, for Christian mission.

Worship and prayer   5min

Choose a worship song to sing together and add the words to the PowerPoint. After the sung worship, pray for God's blessing on the session. If appropriate, ask one or two people in the group to pray.

As an alternative, you could show a clip from the TV news of the day or week, choosing an item that demonstrates our fast-changing world. Ask people to tell their neighbour what their instinctive reaction is to this news item. Suggest that all our responses and reactions can be brought to God who has compassion for the world. Following that, choose a song to sing together that reflects this compassion.

Section two: the church's response to uncertainty

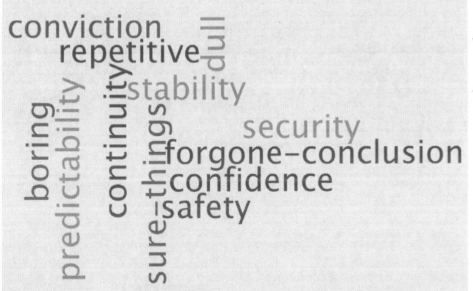

Exploring uncertainty

5min (3min) 💬

Some eras of history seem very stable and certainty seems to rule. A job for life, public schools, English village life, Woolworths! The kind of life and living as most would prefer it - everything in its right place, unchanging and understood. It is easy to plan when we are certain about things. Often many of us try to avoid uncertainty.

 What does certainty feel like? What are the keywords for certainty?

Consider the word cloud (on the slide, in the workbooks and to the left).

You will see that for some, certainty is not necessarily a good thing.

Ask the group for suggestions of other words or feelings.

Sometimes certainty evaporates or is just not attainable. In history, there have been great periods of turmoil eg. in war, in recession and financial crisis, in times of political revolution. There have also been exciting times of discovery and change.

What does uncertainty feel like? What are the keywords for uncertainty?

Consider the word cloud (on the slide, in the workbooks and to the left).

Ask for other suggestions.

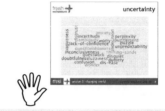

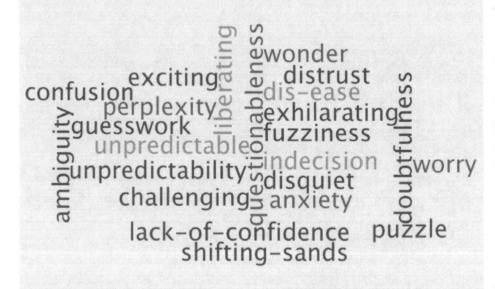

Uncertainty is a dominant feature of our time. Change has been a constant in human history but the pace and extent of change have never been greater. This brings both challenges and opportunities.

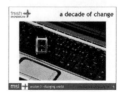

Group exercise

10min (7min)

This exercise aims to explore a loss of certainty of the past ten years. In your groups, please come up with examples of things that have happened over the past decade which have made people less certain about their lives in an unhelpful way.

Possible answers could include:

- employment - no longer a 'job for life', short term contracts;

- politics - in some parts of the world at least, changing politics and changing national regimes;

- security - terrorism threatens national and personal security;

- safety - 'I don't feel safe out late at night';

- financial - people losing their pensions or getting them when older, the value of their investments, their income, student fees, debt;

- relationships - everything more temporary, eg. marriage, family;

- sexuality - some people now ask 'where are you on the gender continuum?';

- technology - rapid and constant change, leads to insecurity and uncertainty around technology;

- theology - no single teaching for all Christians, for all time (eg. Roman Catholic Magesterium) - Rob Bell's book 'Velvet Elvis' says that theology is like trampolining - the springs stretch;

- other - natural disasters.

Our response to uncertainty 15min (13min) 💬

Uncertainty is clearly a negative thing when it:

- makes us take dangerous risks: personal safety, gambling, recklessness;
- leads to a lack of emotional security: being uncertain of self-worth or of being loved.

But as we noted in the word clouds, uncertainty is not necessarily a bad thing. It can be a good thing when it:

- challenges us to think and work hard;
- develops our 'creative' muscles;
- awakens us: our church (or other organisation), uncertain of its future or if it will have one, may be challenged to mission and necessary change;
- allows mystery and wonder - so much a part of our Christian faith and should not be 'done away with' by neat and certain formulae;
- leads us to recognise our need of God.

Many organisations are built to last with certainty and continuity as assumed values. The church of Christendom was built on certainty. We can see this in stone buildings, rule books and authorised texts to name but a few. Is it right to assume that any expression of church should aim to last forever without change? Michael Nazir-Ali, former Bishop of Rochester has said:

> *A faithful Church is continually shaped by its inner dynamic: the flow of Apostolic Tradition, with Scripture as its norm... The Church is, however, also shaped by the kind of world in which it finds itself. This must mean a constant receiving of the Gospel into our particular context.*
> **Michael Nazir-Ali**, Future Shapes of the Church *(House of Bishops paper, 2001) quoted in Mission-shaped Church, p91*

How do people respond to uncertainty? They may:

- panic;
- feel lost or disoriented, clinging to anything that appears solid;
- dig in stubbornly saying 'this is my theory and I'm sticking to it' (as the Monty Python team once said);
- spend! Consumerism becomes a diversion and may appear to offer a form of certainty - 'I shop therefore I am' (there will be more on this in session three);
- opt out - even out of consumerism, perhaps seeing this as no answer, but not seeing any other answer either. This can lead to addictive behaviour and avoidance.

How can we respond to uncertainty in positive ways? We will look at three things:

- what we build;
- how we plan;
- how we think.

Architects have learnt to design flexible buildings for earthquake zones. Can you think of social structures or organisations that do well in less certain times or times of change?

Invite responses. Then give other examples of designed-in flexibility such as the internet, which grew out of a military strategy that realised that if one part of a communication network was destroyed, other parts of a network can take over - data finds alternative routes. This is building for uncertainty.

Simple flexible structures will survive uncertainty better than a fixed institution that cannot adapt quickly.

Some key questions to ponder are:

1. Can we plan well when we can't be sure of anything?

2. What are the better ways to approach mission initiatives and develop fresh expressions of church in uncertain times? We need:

    *   long-term vision, short-term action;

    *   to think big, act small;

    *   to be low on control, high on accountability;

    *   a culture of experimentation, change, adaptation, experimentation and development;

    *   a learning organisation with plenty of review, prayerful action and reflection and the capacity to 'fail forward' by learning from mistakes.

3. People do need fixed points of reference, points of security, familiarity - what are these and how are they expressed in church and Christian community?

4. Could the value of church seasons and rhythms of life be helpfully rediscovered in these uncertain times?

A story

Show either:

*   Cable Street [5.42];

*   The Beacon [8.21].

(In groups) **Discuss how the fresh expression featured is building or planning in an uncertain world.**

It is often said that those who live in the Western world are 'answer-rich but question-poor'. It's a feature of Western culture that we prefer intellectual tidiness and clear-cut answers - systems and certainty. Other cultures cope with greater ambiguity and open-endedness and Jesus himself was 'always with the questions' - a characteristically Jewish approach to teaching.

Answers take us quickly to immediate and specific solutions, which may serve us in the short term. Questions may lead to wisdom, to developing methods of inquiry, equip us in the long term:

- answers are more convergent;

- questions are more divergent;

- answers tend to tell us 'what to think';

- questions tend to help us with 'how to think'.

Ask participants to consider (3min):

Many Christians wear a bracelet asking 'What Would Jesus Do?' But is Jesus the answer or is Jesus the question? Should we wear the bracelet 'What Would Jesus Ask'?

The next two slides take us through a couple of biblical texts which offer encouragement in an uncertain world.

John 14.5-6. End this slide saying the following (or similar):

We are followers of Jesus - 'I am the way'; trusting Jesus - 'I am the truth'; secure in Jesus - 'I am the life'. Jesus is our emotional and spiritual bedrock.

Hebrews 11.1-2. End this slide saying the following (or similar):

'Faith' involves not knowing all that is ahead, yet trusting the person you follow. 'Faith' necessarily involves uncertainty.

2. changing world, changing church

Group exercise   10min (7min) 👥

In your groups, imagine you are meeting with a group of people exploring the Christian faith. In the news that week there has been a major event that has shaken people (it could have been a financial collapse or a natural disaster or some other unforeseen event). Conscious that people will be mindful of this event, prepare an outline for the meeting in which you will explore either John 14.5-6 or Hebrews 11.1-2. No 20-minute sermons allowed! Invite feedback if time allows.

Pause for prayer   5min 💬

Almighty God, you alone can bring order to our unruly wills and affections; give us grace to love what you command and desire what you promise, that in all the changes and chances of this uncertain world, our hearts may surely there be fixed where true joys are to be found: through Jesus Christ our Lord who is alive with you and the Holy Spirit, one God now and for ever. Amen. (New Zealand Prayer Book, p640b)

Choose a suitable worship song and add the words to the PowerPoint slide.

Tre Sheppard
At the foot of the cross
Thankyou Music, 2002

As an alternative, you could show images of crosses from your locality and around the world, both simple and ornate, for personal wear and in public space, used for devotion and worn as fashion. Play a suitable piece of music and ask people to reflect on the place and importance of the cross for them. Then ask people to talk with their neighbour how the cross might be understood in our changing world.

Section three: thinking about networks

Introduction to networks   10min (5min) 💬

Once upon a time, there was something of a battle to get the Bible and public acts of worship changed from Latin into English, the ordinary language of people. This was, of course, so that the Christian faith could be understood and expressed in culturally appropriate ways.

A similar thing is happening today around the forms of church - these need to be appropriate to people, to their cultures, to the way people live and relate to one another today. Increasingly, many people are forming relationships through the networks they belong to, rather than through the geographical areas in which they live.

Think about the networks you know and maybe love!

- the internet - supremely - a network of networks;
- the network of parents and children around school communities;
- networks you join for information or mailings;
- networks around interests, professions or sports.

We need to understand the way our society engages with networks and how church can be missional within that. Eddie Gibbs, in his book *I believe in Church Growth* comments:

In Britain denominational planning has depended too exclusively on the "geographical map". Within the Church of England this has been influenced by the parish structure from rural society with a feudal structure. While the geographical map may be helpful to ensure a measure of blanket coverage, it can at the same time be misleading if used as the only planning model.
Eddie Gibbs, I believe in Church Growth, *p95*

---

2. changing world, changing church

When we talk about 'network society', we mean the way that people live and connect to one another.

Here's an example of a person living within multiple networks - based on a real person, name changed!

Let me tell you about David.

- David lives at - well I won't give his actual address. It's where he eats and sleeps, stores his 'stuff' and meets the neighbours.
- But David works in an office - he is an editor and is well known within the publishing world.
- David also goes to the gym - swims every day, plus various evening groups. He talks to people (not everyone does this) and knows many people in the gym.
- He enjoys the arts and has friends at the theatre - Stratford on Avon.
- He cycles around the country, again meeting up with friends.
- So where does David live? - I might state his address, but where he lives is so much more than that! David lives in all these networks and more. Around every one of David's interests there is a network.

Christians are called and sent to people wherever they live. That's what mission is. If people live in networks, not only in geographical districts or parishes - then these networks need a Christian presence and Christian community.

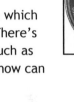

People networks are all about relationships and ways in which people connect to and communicate with each other. There's been a huge rise in the use of social networking sites such as Facebook and Twitter. If we are interested in mission, how can we not engage with this phenomenon?

Of course we don't have to connect with anybody - it's our choice - but Christians need to accept that the kingdom will not grow, nor will we grow personally if we remain in isolation - unlinked to others outside of church. We can't have intimacy with God unless we are involved within the world. We all need inner renewal and outward engagement.

We are sent amongst people with the gospel message (cross-cultural mission) - to connect in appropriate ways:

Now the eleven disciples went to Galilee, to the mountain to which Jesus had directed them. When they saw him, they worshipped him; but some doubted. And Jesus came and said to them, 'All authority in heaven and on earth has been given to me. Go therefore and make disciples of all nations, baptizing them in the name of the Father and of the Son and of the Holy Spirit, and teaching them to obey everything that I have commanded you. And remember, I am with you always, to the end of the age.'
Matthew 28.16-20

Network church is not so much a model of church; it's more of an approach, a mindset.

Some churches are known as 'network churches'. This is what we are inclined to do; put church in a conceptual box and label it. It's tidy and easy to understand, but reality is often more complex and so a mindset mentality is more helpful.

Identifying networks we belong to 10min (5min) 👥

Invite people to get into small groups of three or four, and to record on the large sheets of paper the networks they are part of. Each person should add one network at a time by drawing a dot and labelling it. When they name their next network, they should draw a line from their first dot to their second, but they can also link to other people's dots. So a small group may find that some members have the same gym in common, or a school, or an interest. It's interesting to see how connected people can be!

If there is time, invite people to think about how they could connect missionally with those networks.

Responding to networks 15min ⊘ 👥

We're now going to see another example of a fresh expression of church.

Show one of the following clips:

*   Tubestation [7.12];
*   Riverforce [5.16];
*   Harvest New Anglican Church [7.18].

Invite responses and discuss.

Section four: more about mission

Last time, we thought a fair amount about mission. We want to build on those thoughts as we think about how we might respond to uncertainty and networks in our society.

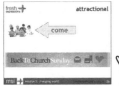

A new way of thinking about mission
5min 💬

Fresh expressions involve a new way of thinking about mission.

We have often operated in an attractional way, inviting people to come and join us. This can still be a fruitful form of mission as Back to Church Sunday has proved.

At other times we have used an engaged method of mission, getting out into our communities, serving people there and then inviting them to come and join us. Again this is still effective in many places with the HOPE Together initiative being a good example.

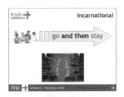

Fresh expressions are fundamentally about an incarnational approach - we go to where people are and stay there, seeking to form Christian community in a new place.

Stop starting with the Church

This short film illustrates this new way of thinking.

 Show the short film *Stop starting with the Church* by Peter Dominey and Kezia M'Clelland of churchfromscratch.org [1.57].

The reality is not as tidy as the last three slides may suggest, and all three approaches are appropriate in different contexts. The important point is that traditionally, being attractive was emphasized most, but that fresh expressions of church place an emphasis on, and are shaped by, an incarnational understanding of mission allowing church to form where people are.

Church for my friend   20min (10min) 👥

Individually, think of a friend who is not part of a church community. Bearing in mind all that we have said, what would a church where your friend feels welcome and at home look and feel like? How might they get involved? When and where would it meet? What kind of opportunities for gathering might it provide? What might happen there?

That's not to say that each person can expect a church that is tailor-made for them, or that panders to their taste. But if we were to start with this person and with what God is doing in their life, what kind of church might we end up with?

When you have considered these questions, share your thoughts in twos, or if you are with a group from your church, that group.

Allow discussion for five minutes or so, and then invite feedback and questions.

Acknowledge that the group has only had a short amount of time for this exercise, but it's designed to get their minds working and their imaginations stimulated.

Closing prayer and worship   5min 💬

Choose a worship song to close the session and add the words to the PowerPoint.

Before singing the song, invite people to close their eyes and to be still for a few moments, to bring all that they have heard and thought before God. Worship together in song and then close the session in prayer.

♪ Geoff Bullock
Lord, I come to you
Word Music/Maranatha Music, 1992

Recommended resources

☑ As an alternative, you could invite people to offer short, simple prayers of thanksgiving for the Church that has nurtured us up to this point - and then to offer short, simple prayers for the Church that will engage lovingly and creatively with the world from this time on. These prayers could be spoken out loud or written onto a large piece of paper or whiteboard.

Finish

Thank people for coming, point out the book recommendations on the handout and confirm the arrangements for the next session.

 Fresh expressions reach out to post-modern society
freshexpressions.org.uk/guide/about/why/postmodern

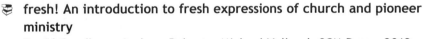

 ### Recommended resources

📖 **fresh! An introduction to fresh expressions of church and pioneer ministry**
David Goodhew, Andrew Roberts, Michael Volland, SCM Press, 2012, 978-033404387-4

📖 **Church Unplugged: Remodelling Church Without Losing Your soul**
David Male, Authentic, 2008, 978-185078792-1.

📖 **Changing World, Changing Church**
Michael Moynagh, Monarch Books, 2001, 978-1854245168.

📖 **Church after Christendom**
Stuart Murray, Paternoster, 2005, 978-184227292-3.

3. re-imagining church - community

Introduction

Aim

To explore the need for fresh expressions of church to develop authentic community in a world shaped by consumerism and individualism.

Outline and timings

These notes are written as a script which you can use 'as is' or adapt to your own needs and experiences. Text in this type is notes for the leader, not to be read out.

The material is designed for a two hour session with the times given in the 120min column to the right. To reduce to a 90 minute session we suggest using the timings in the 90min column, or adapting the material yourself to suit the emphasis of your group.

Re-imagining church - community		120min	90min
Section one: welcome, introductions and worship		**20min**	**7min**
Introduction, recap sessions one and two	💬	2min	2min
Worship and prayer	🙏	5min	5min
Section two: belonging		**20min**	**13min**
Belonging	💬	8min	8min
Where do you belong?	👥	5min	5min
Section three: consumerism, good or bad?		**25min**	**20min**
Me spirituality	💬+⊘(optional)	12min	12min
Story	⊘+👥	13min	8min
Section four: what kind of community?		**55min**	**40min**
Rewriting Acts 2	💬+👥	15min	10min
Pause for prayer	🙏	5min	5min
Community within the church	💬	10min	10min
How can we do this?	👥	10min	* 0min
Open to the community around us	💬	5min	5min
How can we do this?	👥	10min	* 10min
* Combine these two sections into one 10min session at the end of section 4			
Section five: final worship		**20min**	**10min**
Worship and prayer	🙏	20min	10min

Session checklist

Media

Equipment to show clips - laptop, projector, DVD player, TV as required.

Optional: The song *Price Tag* by Jessie J.

Optional: Section three video clips. Purchase these in advance from 'SermonSpice' if you want to use one or both (you can preview them before you buy): *MeChurch* (sermonspice.com/product/413/mechurch) and/or *It's all about me* (sermonspice.com/product/592/It's%20All%20About%20Me).

From the course DVD, one of:

- Somewhere Else [5.46]
  chapter 8 from *expressions: the dvd - 1*
- Zac's Place [6.44], chapter 28 from *expressions: making a difference*

Reflective music and means of playing it, for breaking and sharing bread.

Any song words required.

Other materials

Four large sheets of flipchart paper with one word written in the centre of each: Public, Social, Personal, Intimate. Put these out on tables or stick on the walls so that people can circulate and add things to them. Marker pens.

Your own version of Acts 2.42-47 if required.

Appendix 1 (p129) photocopied and cut up.

A bread machine and bread ingredients. Start baking so that the bread is ready an hour before the session end and will have cooled enough to eat in the final worship. There will be a wonderful smell during the session! If you do not have access to a bread machine, buy some good quality bread instead.

Percussion instruments or noisy objects for the final worship if required.

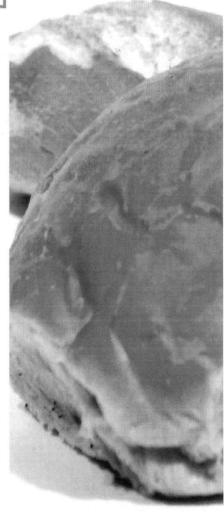

Section one: welcome, worship and belonging

Welcome   2min 💬

Welcome people. Comment on the aroma of baking bread (if you are doing this). Give a quick recap of the material so far:

*   In our first session we considered the *Mission-shaped Church* report and its impact;

*   In the last session we looked at our changing world and the way the church needs to respond.

*   In this time together we are going to reflect on the importance of authentic and deep Christian community in a world shaped by consumerism and individualism.

Worship and prayer   5min 💬

Choose a worship song to sing together and add the words to the PowerPoint. Look for a song that is an expression of communal worship - using 'we' and 'us' rather than 'I' or 'me'. If there is someone gifted in leading unaccompanied singing, this can emphasise our togetherness.

After the sung worship, pray for God's blessing on the session. If appropriate, you could ask one or two people in the group to pray.

Section two: belonging

Belonging

8min

How would you answer the question, 'Where do you belong?'? Your answer might be: 'It depends!' At heart all of us want to feel that we belong somewhere, but in reality we can have a different sense of belonging in different places. The anthropologist Edward T Hall talked about four arenas in which human beings can have a sense of belonging: public, social, personal and intimate space.

1. Public space

Belonging to something 'big', where you feel anonymous and safe. For example, supporting a football club; shopping at Sainsbury's; being a member of a political party; identifying with a particular denomination - 'I'm a Methodist'. In each of these spaces, we can feel a sense of belonging and being at home, of familiarity with our surroundings. But we don't necessarily interact with other people, or have any demands made on us in these spaces. Jesus was a Galilean and would have fitted in with others in the community. He went to the synagogues just like others and to the temple as a young boy, although he would not remain just one of the crowd for very long.

2. Social space

Think of the well-known TV pubs Rovers Return on Coronation Street and EastEnders' Queen Vic - this is social space. Social spaces are where we interact with friends - where 'everybody knows your name'. For example, the local gym if you chat to people there; clubs or pubs that you go to regularly; interest groups or evening classes where you interact with fellow participants; a course like this. In social space we share information about ourselves with our social friends; our interests, opinions, thoughts on the game or latest film but we will probably not share emotionally. Jesus shared social space at the wedding at Cana and with tax collectors and prostitutes!

3. Personal space

This is belonging through close relationships with friends and family - people that you have shared a lot with because of the length of time you have known them, or the things you have experienced together. These are the people who know you well, whom you can relax and be yourself with, whom you can be vulnerable with.

The twelve disciples spent over three years with Jesus following him everywhere and they must have all got to know each other very well in personal space. A good home group or cell group can enjoy personal space.

4. Intimate space

You may have close friends and family in personal space, but still hold back from sharing with them the most difficult things about your life and yet you may need to share this with someone for prayer or support. In intimate space, we can share anything and everything about ourselves with someone else, either because of our depth of trust and friendship or because we have formed a 'contract' to share with each other. Some churches offer this as 'triads' or prayer triplets where one person shares about themselves, a second listens and a third prays in silence.

Perhaps Jesus had such a relationship with the disciples, Peter, James and John. He certainly did with his Father in prayer.

Where do you belong?   5min 💬

Point out the four sheets of paper. Invite people to write on the relevant places where they feel they belong. For 'Intimate space', those who do not want to name names can use symbols or pseudonyms instead. Read out a few examples for each type of space. Tell people you will return to this idea shortly.

Section three: consumerism, good or bad?

Me spirituality

12min 💬 💿

Some people think that changes in culture are responsible for a decline in community. At the root of a lot of the changes in the West (and increasingly other emerging economies) is the rise of consumerism - and the increased choices it brings in every area of life. And what choices we have now on offer.

When I go to a UK supermarket to buy carrots, I can be faced with a choice of 20 different kinds! Do I buy fresh, loose carrots, or pre-weighed in bags, and then what size bag should I get? 200g? 500g? 1kg? or 2.5kg bags? Do I buy organic, or the top of the range superior flavour extra special variety? I can buy whole baby carrots ready prepared, cut into batons or julienne strips, or in a tub with a pot of hummus to dip them in. I can buy them tinned, frozen, juiced, bunched or mashed, in soups, cakes, baby food and even cat food.

It is not surprising if parents lose their cool when children object to eating carrots after all the work parents have put in to buying them!

But choice is not only available in the supermarket. There is overwhelming choice in every area of life: choice about how you live, who you live with, what you do in your spare time, where you work, and how you spend your money.

In contrast to society, which has encouraged choice, the church has historically often limited choice, praised conformity and frowned on individualism. 'We will all stand for the next hymn'. We need to consider how the culture of church feels to someone who is very at home in a consumer culture, where they are encouraged to do what suits them.

So is culture a friend or a foe? The answer is 'both'. We need to learn to critique culture, to decide when to embrace it and when to challenge it.

And in this we can follow the example of Jesus. He was born and brought up within Jewish culture and was a master of discernment, knowing when to work within the culture - and knowing also when to be counter-cultural and challenge the accepted view. We need to be aware of how others are embracing or critiquing culture.

In 2011 the singer Jessie J released the song *Price Tag*, the lyrics of which challenged consumerism. It became a massive hit. The song contained these words:

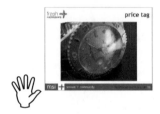

It's not about the money, money, money
We don't need your money, money, money
We just wanna make the world dance, forget about the price tag.
Why is everybody so obsessed? Money can't buy us happiness
Can we all slow down and enjoy right now, guarantee we'll be feelin' all right.
Jessie J, Price Tag

If you have time you might want to play the song.

Despite songs such as Price Tag and the protestors who camped outside St Paul's Cathedral and other locations in 2011, we still live in an age where 'I want' is a dominant theme. 'I want what I want' combines with 'Satisfy me! Satisfy me!' and produces the passive consumer. Consumers issue their demands, hold out their credit cards and wait to be fed with the products they fancy. Passive consumerism can be a real problem.

'Satisfy me! Satisfy me!' is not a stranger to the church!

If you have purchased *MeChurch* or *It's all about me*, play the clip here.

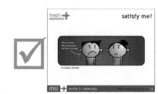

Many attending church demand to be entertained and are dissatisfied if they are not. A Washington Post article (05/01/03) quoted a US pastor who said:

Worship is a form of entertainment... If people are not entertained, they don't feel that they are participating.
Washington Post, 05/01/03

Churches have often allowed Christians to expect entertaining worship in the style of their choice, whether that be choral evensong or contemporary songs. It has allowed Christians to depend too much on the worship or the minister for their spiritual well being, rather than depending on God or the Christian community.

In this way the Christian's spiritual health becomes the church's responsibility, not something for which individuals are also responsible. So, when things go wrong, they blame the church. There is little sense of co-responsibility, co-production and community when it comes to discipleship.

Consumer values are very me-centred and, if they are not careful, churches can collude with this. Sadly, many believers embrace a self-focused Gospel: 'I am the object of the cross'; 'God loves me'; 'My worship experience is important' or 'It's my healing that counts'. Faith becomes all about 'me' rather than glorifying God and serving others. This reflects today's culture which plays up individualism and downplays community.

Consumer culture does create opportunities for mission and service. Here are a few ways some churches are engaging with those who need serving:

1. Offering Christian Spirituality courses at the local college

The thirst for experience may partly explain the widespread interest in 'spirituality'. If a local further education college offers classes in Aromatherapy, Astrology, Crystal Healing, Indian head Massage, Reiki Healing and Tai Chi, why not 'Christian Meditation' or 'Spirituality looking at the Christian Mystics' - as well?

2. Life coaching

A more fluid society means more choice, which increases the possibility that individuals will make the wrong choice. 'Will it be the right option?', 'Is it the best choice?', 'Will I achieve my hopes?' To minimise risk, individuals are turning to experts to help them choose and get the most out of life - mentors, coaches, parenting courses, dating agencies - with psychological profiling to match couples. Might more churches offer life-coaching?

3. Parenting Classes

The television programme *The House of Tiny Tearaways* has run to many series in the UK. Parenting courses will continue to mushroom. A recent study for the UK government confirmed what most teachers already know - the better the parenting skills of the parents, the better the impact on the learning outcomes for the child. Grow Christian community around the needs of parents and families. One lay leader in Wakefield runs a mums and tots group. Her vision is to offer a parenting course. This could develop into:

*   a series on 'questions children ask' followed by;
*   sessions on 'questions adults ask';
*   help with 'spiritual resources that can help us at home';
*   a course introducing Christianity followed by the Emmaus course.

By the end, if people stayed, she would effectively have a small worshipping congregation. Her aim would not be to encourage them to attend church, but to build church around this new community.

Story 13min (8min)

Many fresh expressions are modelling a way of being church that goes beyond the selfishness of consumerism and reaches those on the edge, helping them feel part of the Christian community.

Play one of:

- Somewhere Else [5.46].

    Six years before Barbara Glasson moved to Liverpool, the Methodist Central Hall had closed. She was a minister without a building or congregation. There had been death, therefore, but could there be resurrection? How would you begin, in that situation, to discover where God was at work? Barbara started by walking the streets and listening to the people in the centre of the city, for a year or more. She attended to the very poorest people, those on the margins and the edge. In her own words, she looked for where God was at work.

    For more, visit freshexpressions.org.uk/stories/somewhereelse.

- Zac's Place [6.44].

    Zac's Place began in the late 1990s when Sean Stillman moved to South Wales and conducted a couple of funerals for members of motorcycle clubs, who in turn began to ask very deep questions and wanted to know more about God, but couldn't see how mainstream church was relevant to them. So Sean booked a function room in a local bar every Sunday night to answer some of these questions and many came including bikers, musicians and those on the fringes of society - the vast majority of whom had very little church connection whatsoever. The gatherings aimed to provide opportunity for expression of and enquiry into the Christian faith in a relaxed pub environment. The format consisted of quality live music and other performance art and straight talking in languages and images that relate at street level.

    For more, visit freshexpressions.org.uk/stories/zacsplace.

Invite people to discuss how the story goes beyond selfishness to loving service.

Section four: what kind of community?

Rewriting Acts 2   15min (10min) 💬 👥

The word 'community' is often used to mean a geographical area - what goes on in a district between homes, school, church, post office, civic agencies, public park etc. But we also use the word 'community' to mean 'the sum of relationships a group of individuals has with one another' or their common experience of sharing together.

So a small group can be a community - and experience community, and so can a church. What kind of community does God call us to?

Read Acts 2.42-47 and in small groups re-write it in its opposite sense.

They devoted themselves to the apostles' teaching and fellowship, to the breaking of bread and the prayers.
Awe came upon everyone, because many wonders and signs were being done by the apostles. All who believed were together and had all things in common; they would sell their possessions and goods and distribute the proceeds to all, as any had need. Day by day, as they spent much time together in the temple, they broke bread at home and ate their food with glad and generous hearts, praising God and having the goodwill of all the people. And day by day the Lord added to their number those who were being saved.
Acts 2.42-47

For example, 'Day by day, as they spent much time together in the temple...' (v46) might become, 'They met together whenever they felt like it'!

Thanks to Kelly Betteridge, formerly of CPAS, for this exercise.

Leaders may want to have their own version to read out. Encourage people to compare what they have written and Acts 2.42-47 with their own experience of church - which most reflects their experience?

Invite people to grab a drink while they do this. After 10min, invite feedback - two or three only. Omit feedback for the 90min version.

Read Acts 2.42-47 again to remind people what it says.

This description of the early church gives a feel for the dynamic in their community. This could be described as 'God's church before we got our hands on it' - a spontaneous expression of church that grew out of the reality of people's relationships with God. Professor James Dunn suggests that whenever we see the church being renewed in mission we see the picture of the church presented in Acts 2.42-47 re-emerging:

> *The portrayal may be somewhat idealized... But anyone who is familiar with movements of enthusiastic spiritual renewal will recognise authentic notes: the enthusiasm of the members of the renewal group, with a sense of overflowing joy (Acts 2.46), desire to come together frequently (Acts 2.44,46), eating together and worshipping (Acts 2.46-47) and including the readiness for unreserved commitment to one another in a shared common life.*
> **James Dunn, The Acts of the Apostles, Epworth, 1996, p34**

When asked how others could start a fresh expression, teenager Ruth at The Bridge in Hinckley said 'talk together, eat together, pray together'. Very good advice!

Pause for prayer   5min 💬

Use these prayers to compare what we are, with the Acts 2.42-47 passage, and repent where we fall short. This could include silence.

You could invite people to write and then read out simple prayers that share a common structure, like 'Help us to move from... towards...'.

Community within the church   10min 💬

The early church was:

*   not over-organised - with room for God to work - it had 'holy chaos'.

*   not too centralised - much activity around homes and ordinary living.

*   simply God's people getting on with being Christians in society.

*   liked by the wider community! Acts 2.47: '...having the goodwill of all the people. And day by day the Lord added to their number those who were being saved.'

This church had rich relationships and a real sense of community between its members - they shared possessions in common; they sold property and possessions to give to people in need. It was a place that people could belong to on a personal and intimate level, to use the categories of belonging that we looked at earlier. It was also open and attractive to the wider community around it - they enjoyed the goodwill of people and others were converted and came to join them. It was a place where people could belong on a social and public level that would draw them in to deeper levels of belonging.

The church needs to be a place where people can belong on all four levels - where there are rich, deep relationships between people, as well as space to build relationships and engage with the community around.

Lesslie Newbigin had something to say about Christian community. He was a missionary and bishop who wrote extensively on the need for Christians to engage in mission in the West.

Definition

hermeneutic
interpretation, explanation, making clear, understanding of.

The only hermeneutic of the Gospel is a congregation of men and women who believe it and live by it. The church is to be the primary agent of mission and if it does not exhibit evident community and transformed lives then any amount of evangelistic events and church projects will have limited credibility.
Lesslie Newbigin, The Gospel in a Pluralist society, SPCK, 2004, p227

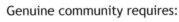

Let's look first at how we can develop rich relationships within Christian community: the personal and intimate belonging that people need to grow into maturity. This is how Jesus said the world would know we were his disciples, by our love for each other (John 13.34,35).

Feel free to add your own stories of good communities and bad communities to illustrate these points.

Genuine community requires:

- honesty: this is so much more than 'not telling lies'. It is about openness, risk and vulnerability. This might be challenging for Christian culture. As is sometimes said, pretending is the common cold of Christianity - everything is wonderful, I'm a great Christian. I have no problems, no doubts, no worries, no issues. Really?

- effort, working at relationships, in particular where they need to be 'sorted' because of a fall out or emotional difficulties, offences caused in the past, bitterness etc.

- reality, which means being unsatisfied by superficiality in relationships - Church should neither be a 'nod at God' nor a 'nod at each other'.

- peace as we discover what it means to be joined together. To share the peace we need to embrace the peace of Christ and live it out.

Refer to Ephesians 4.16:

From whom the whole body, joined and knitted together by every ligament with which it is equipped, as each part is working properly, promotes the body's growth in building itself up in love.
Ephesians 4.16

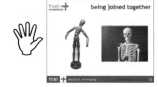

If Paul's metaphor of the body in 1 Corinthians 12 focuses on giftedness and difference, in Ephesians the emphasis is on relationship and community. A bag of bones is not a body! Ezekiel 37 presents an inspiring image of life-giving breath and the joining together, bone by bone, of supporting ligaments.

Our individual giftedness adds to community and mutual service to one another.

Emphasise verses 25 and 26 of 1 Corinthians 12 as examples of strong community in action:

'...so that there should be no division in the body, but that its parts should have equal concern for each other. If one part suffers, every part suffers with it; if one part is honoured, every part rejoices with it.'
1 Corinthians 12.25-26

We won't always get community right, as this slide reminds us. But Christian church ought to be the very best example to the secular world of how it is possible for people to live together. We should be known by our love for each other.

* If running the 90min version, omit this section and combine with the discussion at the end of this section.

How can we do this?   10min (0min*) 👫

Here are some Bible verses that provide guidance for deep and meaningful relationships.

Love one another with mutual affection; outdo one another in showing honour - Romans 12.10

Be kind to one another, tender-hearted, forgiving one another as God in Christ has forgiven you - Ephesians 4.32

Exhort one another every day - Hebrews 3.13

Provoke one another to love and good deeds - Hebrews 10.24

Confess your sins to one another, and pray for one another, so that you may be healed - James 5.16

Bear one another's burdens - Galatians 6.2

Welcome one another - Romans 15.7

Be subject to one another out of reverence for Christ - Ephesians 5.21

Through love become slaves to one another - Galatians 5.13

Bear with one another - Colossians 3.13
Adapted from Phil Potter, The Challenge of Cell Church, BRF, 2001.

 Appendix 1 (p129) is a sheet with these verses on. Copy, cut and give each verse out get those who are able to stand up and read them out in turn. Underline that this theme runs throughout the New Testament.

Open to the community around us   5min 💬

In his book *The Kingdom of God is a party*, Tony Campolo, a sociologist, Christian writer and teacher tells the story of how he was working in Honolulu. Unable to sleep and hungry, he found a diner that was open all night. He sat at the counter eating a doughnut and drinking coffee at 3:30 in the morning when the door opened and in walked a group of prostitutes who were just finishing work for the night. They were dressed provocatively and were loud and boisterous, leaving him quite uncomfortable.

But then he heard one of the women saying to her friend, 'It's my birthday tomorrow'. Her friend replied very scornfully, and the woman said that she had never had a birthday party in her life. Tony decided that he would throw a party for her. He found out that her name was Agnes. He got Harry, the owner of the diner, to help with food and he decorated the diner. By 3.15am the next night the place was full of prostitutes. Then at 3.30am Agnes came through the door and everyone screamed 'Happy Birthday!'. She was stunned, and when Harry produced a birthday cake, she burst into tears. She asked if she could take the cake home to keep her birthday alive for longer. When she left there was a stunned silence in the diner, and Tony took the opportunity to pray for everyone there. He prayed that Agnes' life would be changed and that God would be good to her.

Harry leaned over the counter and with a trace of hostility in his voice, said to Tony, 'Hey! You never told me you were a preacher. What kind of church do you belong to?'

Tony said, 'The kind of church that throws birthday parties for prostitutes at 3:30 in the morning.' Harry said 'No, you don't. There's no church like that. If there were, I'd join it. I'd join a church like that!'

Wouldn't we all?

Church needs to be a place that is open and attractive to the community around it. It needs to provide spaces for public belonging, where people can belong anonymously without commitment being demanded of them.

Cathedrals are a good example of this, seen as tourist sites by those outside the church as much as places of worship. And the church needs to provide spaces for people to belong socially, where people know their name and are pleased to see them.

Somewhere Else/Zac's Place(choose which depending on which you featured earlier) **began by offering this space to** people - a place where they could meet among friends, a place that has drawn people into deeper relationships with each other and with God.

Make the point that we listen not only as a tool of research in order to be successful, but out of concern and love for those we seek to serve. As an example talk about Jesus and the rich young fool where Jesus listened, engaged in conversation, but with no apparent successful result.

To do this, we need to listen to the people in the community around us, just as Barbara Glasson did in Liverpool/Sean Stillman did in Swansea (choose which depending on which you featured earlier).

We need total attentive listening involving:

- listening to God;
- listening to each other;
- listening to those beyond the church.

Brian McLaren offers us a great description of what it means to be a true community within the church:

> *Jesus presents us with a dream (embodied in the group image 'Kingdom of God') that is irreducibly communal, familial and social. It is not just a dream of more and better individual Christians standing like isolated statues in a museum. It is a dream of a community vibrant with life, pulsating with forgiveness, loud with celebration, fruitful in mission... a substantial city whose streets bustle with life, whose buildings echo with praise, a city aglow with the glory of community.*
> **Brian D. McLaren, The Church on the Other Side: Doing Ministry in the Postmodern Matrix, Zondervan, 2002, 978-031025219-1**

How can we do this?   10min (10min*) 👫

Invite people to discuss in small groups:

- What has been the most striking thing you have heard about community tonight?
- Is there one thing you might do to help build community?

Encourage people to share stories of what has worked in their own churches. Invite feedback, although some may have been affected personally and might not feel comfortable sharing widely.

> * If running the 90min version, combine the earlier omitted section with this discussion.

Section five: final worship

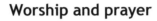

Worship and prayer

20min (10min)

Explain that we are going to take what we have learned and bring it before God.

Read John 15.12-17.

Sing a worship song together. You will need to add the words to the PowerPoint.

During this song, bread from the machine needs to be placed on each table.

Invite people to join in the responses in blue (shown in bold below).

Lord, we are honoured that you call us your friends.
For the lost, the unloved, the marginalised and the victimised
For those in pain, sorrow and grief,
Have mercy, Lord

For those on the edge, not loved and cherished,
Have mercy, Lord
For those in our midst who are lonely and isolated,
Have mercy, Lord

Forgive us Lord when we have squandered opportunities to share your love.
We mourn Lord, for the poverty of our own hearts that would ration out your love.
Have mercy, Lord

And we cry out to you Lord, for the many who are seeking you but take one look at us, the church and run a mile.
Forgive us Lord when we want to settle for the status quo, to take the easy options,
Have mercy, Lord

♪ John Bell, Graham Maule **Song**
Christ's is the world in which we move
Iona Community, 2005

After a short pause, continue:

Jesus told the parable of the yeast to highlight how we must be the growth agent within society. We're now going to share bread together.

In a moment, we invite you to eat from the bread on your table in a small but symbolic prophetic act that God would use us afresh to be his growth agent in our communities: that we may encourage one another, forgive one another, pray for one another, carry each others burdens, accept one another, submit to one another, bear with each other and serve one another in love.

But first let's pray.

Invite people to join in the responses in blue (shown in bold below).

This is your mission Lord, we're in this together!

Blessed are you King of the Universe
who brings forth bread from the earth.
You have given us your peace,
and set a hunger in our hearts.

Restore our strength.
Give new energy to tired limbs, new thought to weary minds.

This is your mission Lord, we're in this together!

As you break off a piece of bread for your neighbour you may wish to say something like:
May you, (Name) be blessed in Christ as you continue to serve Him.

You may wish to then pray silently or audibly for your neighbour.

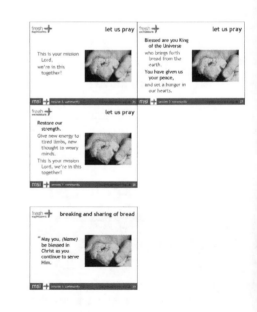

Play reflective music as people share bread together. When everyone has eaten, say this prayer together.

Almighty God,
you call your people to proclaim afresh in every generation
the good news of Jesus your Son.
By the power of your Spirit rekindle in us gifts of courage and
compassion.

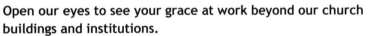

Open our eyes to see your grace at work beyond our church
buildings and institutions.
Help us to work with you in building communities of faith allowing your
mission to be expressed in our hurting world.

May we proclaim afresh your faithfulness and constant love in a changing
and uncertain world.
For the building of your kingdom and to the glory of your name.
Through Jesus Christ our Lord.
Amen.

3. re-imagining church - community

Sing a final worship song. You will need to add the words to the PowerPoint.

Alternatively, for an exercise in communal music-making, provide a variety of things for people to shake, tap and rattle. These could be musical instruments but cartons and boxes can be equally effective and fun to use. Play a piece of music with a strong percussive rhythm in a style that suits your setting. Invite people to join in, quietly at first, then getting progressively louder. Arrange for someone adept at percussion to lead this. They should then lead the group in becoming progressively quieter. Allow a brief silence at the end.

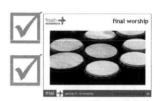

Paul Oakley
Who is there like you?
Kingsway's Thankyou Music, 1995

John Bell, Graham Maule
A Touching Place
Iona Community, 1989

Finish

Thank people for coming, point out the book recommendations on the handout and confirm the arrangements for the next session.

thank you
re-imagining church: community

Recommended resources

 ## Recommended resources

- **Cave Refectory Road: Monastic Rhythms for contemporary living**
  Ian Adams, Canterbury Press Norwich, 2010,
  978-184825028-4.

- **The Hospitality of God**
  Mary Gray-Reeves & Michael Perham, SPCK, 2011,
  978-028106350-5.

- **The Search to belong: Rethinking intimacy, community and small groups**
  Joseph R. Myers, Zondervan, 2003, 978-031025500-0.

- **Through the Pilgrim Door**
  Michael Volland, DC Cook, 2009, 978-184291399-4.

 God works through communities
freshexpressions.org.uk/guide/about/principles/communities

The IN dimension of church
freshexpressions.org.uk/guide/about/proper/in

web

4. re-imagining church - worship

Introduction

Aim

To explore how fresh expressions of church are re-imagining worship.

Outline and timings

These notes are written as a script which you can use 'as is' or adapt to your own needs and experiences. Text in this type is notes for the leader, not to be read out.

The material is designed for a two hour session with the times given in the 120min column to the right. To reduce to a 90 minute session we suggest using the timings in the 90min column, or adapting the material yourself to suit the emphasis of your group.

Re-imagining church - worship		120min	90min
Section one: welcome, introductions and worship		10min	10min
Welcome	🗨	5min	5min
Worship and prayer	🕮	5min	5min
Section two: what is worship?		20min	10min
Draw a chair	👥	10min	5min
What is worship?	🗨+⊘	10min	5min
Section three: re-imagining worship		20min	15min
Creative worship	⊘+🗨	20min	15min
Section four: experiencing creative worship		40min	30min
Worship stations	🕮	30min	25min
Feedback	🕮	10min	5min
Section five: making changes		30min	25min
How can we re-imagine worship?	🗨	10min	10min
Creating worship	👥	15min	10min
Final worship and prayer	🕮	5min	5min

Session checklist

Media

Equipment to show clips - laptop, projector, DVD player, TV as required.

Sister Act clip.

From the course DVD:

*   worship [2.38]

Instrumental reflective music and means of playing it.

Any song words required and information about your opening worship song if required.

Other materials

A few sheets of flipchart paper for each small group, plus marker pens. People will be drawing at the start of the session so it may be easier to have a table to gather around.

Materials for worship stations - see instructions and suggestions on pages 78-81. Six stations are suggested but feel free to create your own. You will need to set up the stations in advance of the session.

Copies of the sheets for the creating worship exercise (appendix 2, pp128-9). Cut the sheets into slips and put each category (senses, objects, seasons) into a separate bowl, enough for each group to have one slip from each of the categories.

Chocolate fountain and chocolate/sweets/fruit to dip, if required.

4. re-imagining church - worship

Section one: welcome, introductions and worship

Welcome   5min 💬

Take time to welcome participants.

Give a quick recap of the material covered so far:

*   In our first session we considered the *Mission-shaped Church* report and its impact;
*   In the second session we looked at our changing world and the way the church needs to respond;
*   In the third session we explored the need for authentic community within church in a consumerist society;
*   In this time together we are going to look at what worship is and how we can creatively re-imagine it for today's culture.

Worship and prayer   5min 🗣

Choose a worship song to sing together and add the words to the PowerPoint.

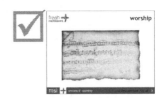

Discover beforehand the story of this particular song and the tradition from which it comes and tell that story very briefly. Point out the authenticity of the song in its context. Float the idea that the theme of the song might be expressed very differently in other settings.

After the sung worship, pray for God's blessing on the session. If appropriate, you could ask one or two people in the group to pray.

Section two: what is worship?

 ### Draw a chair 10min (5min) 👫

Invite one or two people at each table or group to draw a chair. Encourage them to fill the paper. Get each person to stand and show the room their chair.

Comment on the pictures. If they are all very different, affirm them for representing the diversity of chairs! If they are all similar, point out that chairs can in fact be very different to each other.

This simple exercise challenges our preconceptions of how we define and understand worship. We may all use the same word but do we all picture the same thing when we say the word 'worship'?

 ### What is worship? 10min (5min) 💬 💿

This course is about 'changing minds, changing church'. Worship is only one aspect of church life, but it is a very important one. What happens when we gather together says a lot about the God we worship and our values as a church. There are many different forms, styles and expressions of worship. Is the expression of worship we are used to just our way of doing things? Is it the only way?

We can often make worship be about what we like or prefer. It can be more about me and satisfying my wants and needs than about loving and serving God (a consumerist attitude). Sadly, that which should draw us together has often split us apart in painful arguments about style and content. So how different could worship be from that with which we are familiar?

4. re-imagining church - worship

In the first session we saw a clip from Sister Act where the choir-led worship was quite painful. The film goes on to explore what might happen to a church where the worship in church is revitalised and expressed through people's lives as the members reconnect with the community. Obviously this is a Hollywood version of reality, but as you watch this clip, reflect on whether there is any truth in it. In the film, Sister Mary-Clarence, played by Whoopi Goldberg, takes over the choir. The change in quality and passion is dramatic, but the Mother Superior is incensed at what she sees as blasphemy and calls Sister Mary-Clarence into her office for a telling-off!

The clip starts at the beginning of chapter 18 (0:55:30), the nuns huddled outside Mother Superior's office to hear what she is saying. It ends when Mother Superior looks out of her office at what the sisters are doing in the community (1:00:40).

If you have time, you could start at chapter 17, which includes the revamped choir that has caused the Mother Superior such angst. This adds 3:50 to the clip.

So what is worship? It is so much more than services, songs, sermons and sacrament. We are called to offer the whole of our being and the whole of our life to God, through our loving, serving, offering and worship. Worship is a way of life that is offered and renewed in specific activities, both personal and corporate. Life and worship should be entirely mixed and inter-mingled, woven together. On that basis, the mission we are involved in is worship - and worship renews mission.

At the heart of mission is a call to worship as part of a community - but in our changing society with changing Sundays, changing relationships, changing culture and with less knowledge of faith, what sort of worship gathering will be authentic and real in the 21st century?

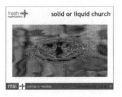

There is so much that could be said about worship. There are substantial challenges and fantastic opportunities to work through. A helpful book on this subject is Pete Ward's book Liquid Church where he sets out an interesting thesis on how the church can embrace the liquid nature of culture rather than just scrambling to keep afloat.

Solid church is based on the assumption that it is good for large numbers of very different people to meet in the same room and do the same sort of thing together.

In the BBC game show *The Weakest Link* contestants were asked questions in turn. A correct answer earned a certain amount of money, but this money had to be banked if it was to form part of the eventual prize. Solid church has its eyes firmly on the bank. People may have turned to Christ through the youth mission or Alpha course, and this is good, but if they are not banked, they don't really count, until they start to attend Sunday services.

We must ask ourselves about the key values of our churches, because they will partly determine our styles of worship. Certain things have happened in the history of your church that makes it function in a particular way - are these still helpful to your community or are they out-dated?

A curate from a growing market town church started a 'fresh expression' for the unchurched in that town to which 30-40 people went regularly on a Tuesday night. Set up in an attractive church hall with settees and comfy armchairs, people were invited to meet for drinks, nibbles, chat, questions on various themes with discussion groups, pre-alpha materials, film clips and a weekly fun quiz. Its popularity grew. People were making commitments to follow Christ, and there were a number of baptisms.

Over a short period of time, the word was out that Tuesday nights were a fun place to get together and gradually, the disaffected Christians and those on the fringe started to turn up in force. Gradually, the evening started to take the shape of Sunday church and the original unchurched people felt their group was being hijacked and started to leave. The curate saw this happening and separated the groups again, but some were really cross and never came again. Eventually the vicar pulled the plug on this fresh expression expressly saying that he wanted his curate to run Alpha and then get people in on a Sunday morning where they would receive teaching together all at the same time. This is solid church in action and it still works for some people. However, only four or five people made the jump from the Tuesday night group to Sunday church. The curate was due to move on five months later and now the group has closed.

Pete Ward says that one of the unseen key values of solid church is this 'one-size-fits-all' environment and that even worship must fit in with that. As a result we sometimes provide a bland and inoffensive diet of middle-of-the-road music and safe spirituality. Variety is discouraged and extremes are tempered because a key value is that we do not offend anyone who comes to church regularly. One or two critical comments will prompt the leaders of the church to tell the youth group to turn the instruments down!

The church must be like water - flexible, fluid, changeable.
Pete Ward

Ward urges us to move away from the traditional notion of church as a gathering of people meeting in one place at one time to the dynamic notion of church as a series of relationships and communications. However, it depends on what sort of culture we find ourselves in. If your culture warms to regular gatherings, a solid expression of church is appropriate. As people live more fluid lives, the church needs to be more flexible too.

Creative worship

20min (15min)

Many fresh expressions of church are experimenting with creative worship which is integral to their life and mission. This clip shows a variety of worship styles from fresh expressions of church around the country.

 Show the worship montage clip [2.38].

Creative worship will look different in different contexts as you would expect, but there are some common themes. The images are from Grace, an alternative worship community which is a congregation of St Mary's in Ealing.

 ### Creative worship... reframes tradition

When developing worship, it is important to be rooted in the Christian tradition and in the Word of God. Rather than starting completely from scratch, many fresh expressions are revisiting the traditional worship of the church and reframing it for our own culture. *Grace* has a Lent service every year, for example and runs a Lent blog that members of the community contribute to, with a thought for each day (the slide image is of ash, used at Lent).

Bishops Michael Perham and Mary Gray-Reeves suggest that:

> *[the greatest gift fresh expressions can offer to the whole church is a] sense of confidence in what we have been given and its potential to draw us and others more effectively into the experience of the love and beauty and holiness of God. Such confidence will make us more creative and more adventurous in our worship and will allow the grace of God to be experienced both in the traditional things we shall do better and in the new things we shall do well.*
> **Michael Perham, Mary Gray-Reeves, The Hospitality of God, SPCK, 2011, p146**

Creative worship... uses contemporary culture

Groups may create environments, using contemporary culture in local contexts, which will feel familiar and are not an alien experience for those outside the church. For example, using beanbags to sit on, visuals, film, low lighting, contemporary music with spiritual themes alongside explicitly Christian music.

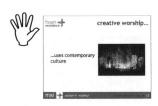

This is a typical set up for *Grace*. Much equipment is borrowed or has been accumulated over the years - you don't need a massive budget to start. Be creative with what you have and develop your magpie tendencies, looking out for things in everyday life that you can use in worship.

Creative worship... is multi-sensory

In planning worship, groups may think about how the experience will impact different senses - sight, sound, smell, touch and taste. This multi-sensory approach can encourage participants to be open to God in new ways and provide a multi-faceted worship experience rather than a one-size-fits-all approach.

At Pentecost, *Grace* did a service on the theme of the Spirit which started with a multi-sensory walk down the side of the church. People removed their shoes and were blindfolded, making their way down the side of the church, treading on different textures and feeling them on the walls, smelling cut lemons and an oil burner, feeling a fan blowing and so on. As we cannot see the Spirit of God we may need to sense the Spirit in different ways; this walk enabled people to think about how they might do that.

Creative worship... is participative

Worship is not about an audience being entertained. Rather than having a worship leader who leads publicly from the front, many groups actively encourage all members to participate in creating worship. The structure of

services, using stations or interaction, can facilitate this and the ethos of creativity and experimentation means that there are no worship 'experts', just people learning and worshipping together.

Every Christmas, Grace has a service of nine lessons and carols. Members take one of the traditional nine readings and use it as the basis of an activity, meditation or film clip, along with a piece of music. It has been a great way to enable people to participate in creating worship.

Creative worship… is accessible to all

People engage at different levels, for different personalities, moods, life experiences, ages etc.

Many groups have found that children, adults and teenagers can worship together instead of having something separate for those who are younger. There is space for people to be real about the situations and concerns that they bring to worship.

Creative worship… creates space for a response (but not a uniform one)

Groups have rediscovered the importance of ritual to mark events and transitions. Services will often provide space for creative responses that people can engage with at different levels, depending on their own circumstances.

At the Spirit service at *Grace*, people made paper kites and wrote on them their desire to be energised by the Spirit of God, and the hopes and dreams that they wanted to be filled with God's Spirit.

4. re-imagining church - worship

Section four: experiencing creative worship

Worship stations   30min (25min) 💬

Explain that people will have 30min to engage with the worship stations, each of which has a focus and materials to interact with. They can spend all the time at one station if they like, or visit a few. Encourage them to linger at each station and engage with the theme.

You might like to play background instrumental music.

A couple of minutes before the end of the time, ask people to finish what they're doing at the station they are at and return to their seats.

Creating worship stations

A station is a dedicated area that has a focus for worship and prayer. Usually people are given time and space to spend as much time moving around each as they choose.

They are limited only by your imagination, but think multi-sensory. You need enough so that only about six people will be in any one zone at a time. Some can be very simple - a chair, a candle and a Bible for example.

At a station you could have:

- something to watch (a video, a mirror) or read (poetry, Scripture);
- something to smell (fresh flowers, incense);
- something to touch (fabric, dried up leaves);
- something to taste (salt, water);
- something to hear (music, a song);
- something to say (prayer, Bible reading) and so on.

Make your stations visually attractive (this will take time) using:

- fabric: flame-proofed only;
- candles: kept clear of anything inflammable and set on trays or in holders;
- lights;
- bibles;
- sculpture - such as praying hands, figurines;
- natural material - such as wood, cloth, water, sand, pebbles, glass beads.

Give each station a different feel:

- a silent station;
- a station where Bible passages are read out and meditated on;
- a station for spoken prayer;
- a station where reflective music can be heard;
- an activity station (for example, moulding clay into a shape which represents yourself or your feelings about something).

Give each station a different theme. Here are just some examples (there are more detailed examples overleaf):

- The world (map, globe, prayer requests);
- Stillness (candles, quiet music, running water);
- Intercession (prayer requests, candles to light);
- Local community (map, newspapers, photos, rolling PowerPoint);
- Learning (video someone explaining what worship means to them);
- The workplace (work objects: tools, PCs, school books).

Feedback 10min (5min) 💬

Invite people to discuss the experience over drinks. You don't want them to over-analyse what has happened, as they may need time to process it.

Encourage people to say what they found helpful about the stations and how were they enabled to connect with God. Then invite them to say what was not helpful. Encourage people to share stories of other creative worship they have shared in or organised.

Ideas for worship stations

If you have never used stations in worship before, you might like to use or adapt these suggestions. Print each set of instructions onto a card and place with the materials listed at the relevant worship station.

Confessions

'Have our churches become a barrier to people meeting with God? Spend some time in prayer, asking for forgiveness and wisdom. Eat some parsley dipped in salt water as a symbol of confession.'

- sprigs of parsley and a bowl of salt water;
- a Bible open at Isaiah 1.18 or that verse printed on a sheet.

Hopes and dreams

'What are your hopes and dreams for your church? Write them on a piece of paper and spend some time praying about them. Then make your paper into a boat and place it on the mirror, as a symbol of launching your dreams into the kingdom of God.'

- sheets of A4 paper and pens
- some simple origami boats that people can copy;
- a circular mirror to lay on the floor as 'water';
- a Bible open at Joel 2.28-29 or that verse printed on a sheet.

Stillness

'This is a space to rest in the presence of God. A place to be still. A place to listen. A place to just be.'

- some cushions or a rug for people to sit on;
- some Bibles.

Focus on Jesus

'Jesus said, "I am the light of the world." Jesus said, "You are the light of the world." Pray for the light of Christ to shine in your life, in your church, in your neighbourhood. Pray for Christ's light to shine through you. Light a candle to spread the light of Christ.'

- a large lighted candle, secure on a stand;
- small unlit nightlights, on a sand tray or some other safe foundation.

Coping with change

'It's hard to cope with change. Use the play dough to make a symbol of what your church is like. Pray for God to be at work in the hearts of your church members, so that they are open to the change that God wants to bring about. Mould the play dough into a symbol of what you hope your church will become as people listen and respond to God.'

- some pots of play dough and mats or plates for people to make models on;
- a Bible open at Isaiah 64.8 or that verse printed on a sheet.

Local community

'Pray for your local community, that your church may be salt and light in it. Use the pens to highlight the places where you live, work and worship, and the places where you would like to have more impact.'

- a map of the local community: include the places that your participants come from if possible;
- highlighter pens;
- a Bible open at Matthew 9.36-38 or that verse printed on a sheet.

Section five: making changes

How can we re-imagine worship?　　10min 💬

As we've already said, it can be dangerous trying to change the way that worship is done! But it's a risk that might have some surprising outcomes.

One group of Methodist churches took a large room in one of their buildings and transformed it into a creative space for prayer - it was 'liquid prayer' in action where people could write their prayers on the walls, make graffiti art, or pray in a makeshift cage to identify with those imprisoned for their faith.

Surprisingly, those who got the most out of that week of 24/7 prayer were the older people, who had thought they were going to hate it and booked an hour early in the week to get it over and done with. They went just to show willing, but actually encountered the presence of God in a way they hadn't experienced for a long time. Faith was renewed and a desire to be with God was strengthened and encouraged. Many enjoyed it so much that they signed up for more sessions later in the week and brought their friends!

Re-imagining worship is not about superficial changes to church services. Jesus waits for us to stop arguing about styles and tools and to marry our worship with our mission, to work with him in bringing many into the kingdom of God. As we saw in session 3, the early church discovered this:

Day by day, as they spent much time together in the temple, they broke bread at home and ate their food with glad and generous hearts, praising God and having the goodwill of all the people. And day by day the Lord added to their number those who were being saved.
Acts 2.46-47

Worship and mission are inextricably linked. It's about being worshipping, missional communities, where worship and community life are renewed alongside each other. So how can we begin to re-imagine worship?

Start small, start at the edges

Making changes to Sunday morning worship may be too radical for people to cope with. So you could start by introducing new ideas to home or cell groups. You could put on a prayer evening for the church with some new ideas alongside more familiar ways of praying. If there are a number of people who feel the same way, you might want to start a monthly creative worship service, or ask if you can contribute to or re-introduce a Sunday or weekday evening service. Try to find ways for people in the church to experience creative worship rather than just talking about it. If you are starting something new, make sure that the worship reflects the ethos and values of the fresh expression of church from day one.

Create worship from the gifts and resources that you have

Look around those you know to see what gifts people have. They may not be involved in leading worship already, precisely because the style of worship doesn't fit what they have to offer. Are there photographers, artists, DJs, musicians or dancers who might get involved? Take inspiration from other groups but don't copy directly. You need to do what's appropriate for the people involved.

Connect with other groups to see what they do

Bearing in mind what has just been said about not copying, it is useful to connect with and even visit other groups to expand your imagination and to experience new things. Visit freshexpressions.org.uk for some ideas, or ask around your diocese, district, presbytery, synod or network.

Embrace your creativity!

We are all made in the image of our creator God and so are all creative. It's easy to look at what other people do and to think 'I could never do that!' but if we recognise our own creativity, then we'll be freed to try new things.

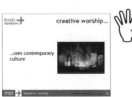

Invite people to share their own experiences of introducing creativity into worship. There is a lot we can learn from each other.

Creating worship   15min (10min)

We're going to do an exercise to come up with creative ideas for worship.

Invite people to work in threes or fours. Each group should take one slip from each of the bowls, so they end up with a sense, an object and a season You could make the objects themselves available (rather than just paper slips) to enable hands-on engagement with the exercise.

Your task is to come up with a creative worship or prayer idea that combines the three elements that you have been given. It may feel a little contrived to be given these parameters, but the reality of creativity is that we often respond well to these kinds of suggestions, rather than starting with a completely blank sheet of paper. You have ten minutes to come up with your idea and then we're going to hear from each group.

After ten minutes or so, invite feedback from the groups. Affirm their ideas and creativity and encourage them to keep thinking creatively.

Final worship and prayer   5min

Close with a simple act of worship that one of the groups prepared earlier - perhaps one related to the current season of the Church year.

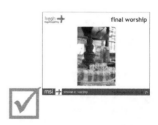

Alternatively, as at least one msi course has done, use a chocolate fountain - a celebratory end to the session, linking in with the discussion around solid and liquid and celebrating the goodness of God who invites us to share in the feast of his kingdom. You could base the worship around 'Taste and see that the Lord is good' (Psalm 34.8).

Close in prayer.

Recommended resources

Finish

 Thank people for coming, point out the book recommendations on the handout and confirm the arrangements for the next session.

 The UP dimension of church
freshexpressions.org.uk/guide/about/proper/up

web

Recommended resources

- **50 Worship Ideas for Small Groups**
  Stuart Townend, Morgan Lewis, Kingsway, 2000, 978-184291279-9.

- **Curating Worship**
  Jonny Baker, SPCK, 2010, 978-028106235-5.

- **Emerging Churches: Creating Christian Communities in Postmodern Cultures**
  Eddie Gibbs, Ryan K Bolger, SPCK, 2006, 978-028105791-7.

- **Messy Church** series
  Lucy Moore, see messychurch.org.uk/pages/3520.htm for details.

- **Creative Ideas for Alternative Sacramental Worship**
  Simon Rundell, Canterbury Press, 2010, 978-184825023-9.

5. re-imagining church - discipleship and leadership

Introduction

Aim

To explore how to enable healthy discipleship and leadership within fresh expressions of church.

Outline and timings

These notes are written as a script which you can use 'as is' or adapt to your own needs and experiences. Text in this type is notes for the leader, not to be read out.

The material is designed for a two hour session with the times given in the 120min column to the right. To reduce to a 90 minute session we suggest using the timings in the 90min column, or adapting the material yourself to suit the emphasis of your group.

Re-imagining church - discipleship and leadership		120min	90min
Section one: welcome, introductions and worship		**10min**	**5min**
Welcome	💬	2min	2min
Worship and prayer	🐑	8min	3min
Section two: valuing creativity		**5min**	**5min**
Made in the image of God	💬	5min	5min
Section three: discipleship		**55min**	**40min**
Thinking about discipleship	💬+⌚	10min	5min
How was it for you?	👥	10min	10min
Developing discipleship in fresh expressions	💬+👥	30min	20min
Pause for prayer or praise	🐑	5min	5min
Section four: leadership - the journey continues		**40min**	**30min**
Introductory comments and DVD	💬+⌚	10min	10min
Leadership in a fresh expression	💬+⌚+👥	30min	20min
Section five: closing meditation		**10min**	**10min**
Spiral galaxy	🐑	10min	10min

Plan well: There is a lot of material to cover. You may wish to spend this session looking at creativity and discipleship, leaving out section four and adding an extra session to the course to cover the material on leadership. This is particularly helpful if you are using the 90min version of the session.

Session checklist

Media

Equipment to show clips - laptop, projector, DVD player, TV as required.

A clip and picture from the week's news for the opening worship, if required.

From the course DVD, one of:
- Zac's Place [6.44], chapter 28 from *expressions: making a difference*
- Cable Street [5.42], chapter 14 from *expressions: the dvd - 1*

From the course DVD:
- *Covenant* by *The Smiling Strangers* [3.17], or other reflective music.

From the course DVD, one of:
- re:generation [6.36], chapter 13 from *expressions: making a difference*
- St George's [6.53], chapter 16 from *expressions: making a difference*

The Wrong Trousers DVD (Park, 1993).

Meditative music and the means to play it, for the closing meditation.

Any song words required.

Other materials

Rucksack and other props, for the discipleship exercise. Suggested props: a Bible; bread; a symbol of prayer, eg. praying hands or a book of prayers; a small cross made of two twigs; some Lego or Playmobile people or a photo of some people you might journey with; newspaper; other symbols of things you think are important for the journey of discipleship.

Sheets of flipchart paper and pens.

Muslin or other material for closing activity in section five, plus luminous stars or counters (around five for each person).

Section one: welcome, introductions and worship

Welcome   2min 💬

Welcome participants and give a quick recap of the material so far in the course:

- In our first session we considered the *Mission-shaped Church* report and its impact;

- In the second session we looked at our changing world and the way the church needs to respond;

- In the third session we explored the need for authentic community within church in a consumerist society;

- In the fourth session we discussed the need to re-imagine worship;

- In this session we will be exploring how we can encourage and enable healthy discipleship and leadership within fresh expressions of church.

Worship and prayer

8min (3min)

 Choose a worship song to sing together and add the words to the PowerPoint.

Pray for God's blessing on the session or ask people in the group to pray.

 As an alternative, you could show a video clip from the TV news of the day or week, choosing an item that includes the actions or words of someone in leadership or learning/discipleship in some arena of life. Put a picture of this person on the slide. Ask people to tell their neighbour what their instinctive reaction is to this type of leadership or learning (positive or negative). Then suggest that all of our responses and reactions can be brought to God who has compassion for us and for the world - and choose a song to sing together that reflects this.

Section two: valuing creativity

Made in the image of God   5min 💬

The first thing we know about God from the Bible is that God is creative. As we have already seen, fresh expressions of church are seeking to reconnect with the creativity of God in mission and worship. Creativity is also important when it comes to forming disciples and encouraging all to exercise appropriate gifts of leadership.

This excellent quote is long and needs to be read well. You may want to shorten it.

Theologian Leonard Sweet describes the old world of modernity and the new world of post-modernity in which we all now exist like this:

> *The modern world was grounded. Its favorite definition of God was 'Ground of Being'. Its basic metaphors were drawn from a landscape consciousness that didn't trust water. Scholars are trained to keep categories clean and 'watertight'. We were taught to avoid watering down our insights. The surface on which we lived was solid, fixed, and predictable. We could get the lay of the land, mark off directions where we were headed, and follow maps and blueprints to get where we were going. Much time, energy, and even spilt blood were devoted to defending, maintaining, and marking off our boundaries. Border disputes were common and devastating.*
>
> *Postmodern culture has marched off all maps. Its environment is a seascape; its surface is fluid and not fixed. It changes with every gust of wind and every wave. It is always unpredictable. Old maps and blueprints are useless on an uncharted, ever changing seascape. The sea knows no boundaries. The only way to get where one is going on a seascape is through nautical skill and trajectories rather than through fixed and clearly identified roads and highways.*

In this world, fluidity wins over fixity. Instead of structuring and ordering and solidifying reality, cyberspace bends and melts it. Life is a fluid realm. Fluid however, does not mean anything goes, as any capable ship captain will quickly affirm. Fluid is a different kind of order, a different kind of going.
Leonard Sweet, Soul Tsunami: Sink or Swim in New Millennium Culture, Zondervan, 1999

Creativity is key to navigating this ever-changing seascape, whether we are navigating as a disciple of Jesus, or in a leadership role helping others to find a way through the seascape.

Let's look at a definition of 'create':

cre•ate tr.v. cre•at•ed, cre•at•ing, cre•ates

1. To cause to exist; bring into being.
2. To give rise to; produce.
3. To invest with an office or title; appoint.
4. To produce through artistic or imaginative effort: create a poem; create a role.

God the Father is our creator, God the Son is the one who calls us to discipleship and God the Spirit is the one who leads the leaders.

Back to our statement of 'ologies' from the first session.

Our theology shapes our missiology which determines our ecclesiology.

Our beliefs about God will affect our understanding of mission which will determine the way we do church, form disciples and grow leaders.

Discipleship was never meant to be dull and formulaic. When Jesus said to the first disciples 'follow me', he was inviting them to a life-changing adventure of risk and discovery. In these days in particular, Christian leadership must involve helping people and communities bring about new things in God. Christian leadership should, in large part, be about fostering, encouraging, enabling creativity in the Christian community.

But does that happen? Does church culture nurture or stifle creativity and freethinking across its wider membership?

Some individuals, artists, liturgists and musicians have been nurtured and commissioned as creative artists for the church or encouraged by the church to use their gifts in mission wherever God has placed them. But in terms of every-member ministry, creativity and freethinking for all has not often been the dominant culture.

Church culture:

- can stifle creativity

    Churches can frame regulations and structures to order its life and protect against error but these can generate a 'can't do' rather than a 'can-do' mindset. People can feel restricted and disempowered.

- or it can foster creativity

    Church must reflect every aspect of the nature of God including God the creator and that aspect of church life should be shaped by permission giving, experimentation, and releasing.

    Creativity should be the norm - not only in worship, but in thinking about forms of church community, mission, prayer - in fact in its whole life as a community, church should be shaped by creativity.

There seems to be a recent surge of creativity in the church and this is a move of the Holy Spirit and not to be quenched.

So as we look at fresh expressions of church and the way in which they encourage the formation of disciples and leaders we need to value creativity.

Leadership for this time of change, and for navigating this seascape, will involve helping people and Christian communities explore their God-given creativity.

We will return to this later, but first we explore the key area of discipleship.

Section three: discipleship

Thinking about discipleship   10min (5min) 💬

Before he returned to be with his father, Jesus gave a Commission to his disciples.

Now the eleven disciples went to Galilee, to the mountain to which Jesus had directed them. When they saw him, they worshipped him; but some doubted. And Jesus came and said to them, 'All authority in heaven and on earth has been given to me. Go therefore and make disciples of all nations, baptizing them in the name of the Father and of the Son and of the Holy Spirit, and teaching them to obey everything that I have commanded you. And remember, I am with you always, to the end of the age.'
Matthew 28.16-20

This is the task that we have inherited, to 'make disciples' of all people - not to count converts, or fill our churches, but to create environments where people grow and develop in their faith, becoming mature, long-term followers of Christ.

1. Discipleship - a journey, not a crisis event

Some forms of mission in the past have focused on events that demand a response - giving people an opportunity to make a decision for Christ at an evangelistic event. While still recognising that people do need to make a decision about following Christ, the emphasis more recently in many parts of the church has been on discipleship as a journey rather than a crisis event.

Think of Peter. When did he become a disciple? At the lakeside when he first heard Jesus say 'follow me' (Mark 1.17)? Or when he professed Jesus to be the Christ (Matthew 16.16)? Or when Jesus restored him after his denial (John 21.19)? Or when he was filled with the Spirit at Pentecost (Acts 2.4)? All of these were mighty moments for Peter but it all began with curiosity.

Very often people are growing in relationship with Christ, in discipleship, before they make a public Christian commitment - and they need to continue to grow afterwards! What matters most is people's living relationship with God now, not whether they went forward at an evangelistic event in the past.

2. Believe; behave; belong and bless?

In the past, some churches expected certain standards before people were fully welcomed as members of the church. The emphasis was on 'believe; behave; belong'. Or in other words, 'You need to believe the same as us; you need to behave to our standards and then we will let you belong to our community'.

Christian youth workers in particular have found a different emphasis to be much more effective in making disciples: 'belong; believe; behave'. They allow young people to belong to the group regardless of their beliefs, sharing life, learning and worship with Christians. Once these young people have a sense of belonging, they have a safe space to ask questions, to learn and grow, and then often they will come to believe in Jesus. Once they have had an encounter with Jesus, their behaviour will begin to change as they are transformed by the Holy Spirit.

From your experience you may want to put the words in a different order, with a slightly different understanding of the word 'behave'. The model could now be 'belong; behave; believe'. People are welcomed as part of the community and encouraged to behave like followers of Christ, taking part in worship (as appropriate) and service alongside other Christians in the community even if they are not yet committed believers; and they will then come to a place of belief in Jesus and a relationship with him.

Stephen Lindridge, Fresh Expressions Connexional Missioner for the British Methodist Church, suggests a fourth 'b' is key to forming disciples, namely blessing. He suggests that by the work of the Holy Spirit through ordinary and extraordinary encounters with Jesus, people can respond to God's love with no real beliefs in place, without belonging to a group of believers or without even being moral in their values and practice. However, it is through blessing that they experience something of the reality of God. God breaks into their lives and they respond to a journey towards a relationship with Jesus (William Porter, *Igniting Leadership*, Moorleys, 2005, p125-30).

What is important in all of these possible pathways is that we form welcoming communities, accept people as they are and recognise that God is at work in them as much as he is in us. However people come to be Christian disciples, what is absolutely clear from both Church history and healthy fresh expressions of church is that they grow best in community.

Case study

Show one of:

- Zac's Place [6.44];
- Cable Street [5.42].

These stories show how fresh expressions of church are inviting people to belong first and then believe and behave as they are blessed.

3. What sort of journey?

If discipleship is a journey, what sort of journey is it? We do need to be careful with language as for some the word journey has become synonymous with celebrity culture, with many an X-Factor wannabe giving thanks as they sob to all those, from their Mum to Cheryl Cole, who have helped them on their journey to their five minutes of fame.

The Christian journey of discipleship is a journey that begins in response to the call of Jesus to 'follow me'. That call can come in many different forms. For some it may come very directly with a profound sense of the Lord calling. For many it comes when a Christian friend offers an invitation to join their group. For others it comes gradually as they realise that Jesus is real and loves them too. For still others it comes when they meet Christ in the form of the poor and needy and, without knowing, minister to him or vice versa.

How did the journey begin for you?

Above all else, Christian discipleship is a journey to Christ-likeness (2 Corinthians 3.18, Ephesians 4.13 and 1 John 3.3). Then discipleship is:

* a lifelong apprenticeship - Jesus himself knew the value of being apprenticed, growing up in a carpenter's shop;

* lived out in the whole of life, not just the 'churchy' bits - a Christian midwife is as much a disciple when she is delivering babies as when she is leading the worship group;

* an adventure - we may not know where we are going but we know who we are going with;

* communal - disciples grow through supportive relationships. Jesus himself modelled this with different forms of relationships: His closest companions - Peter, James and John, his small group - the twelve, then the wider circle of women and men who shared his life and mission;

- biblical - the written word draws us to and guides us in the ways of the living word;

- cross-shaped - the call of Jesus is cruciform, costly and sacrificial - Luke 9.23 says 'if any want to become my followers, let them deny themselves and take up their cross daily and follow me';

- sacramental - true discipleship is marked by the sacrament of baptism, nurtured by the sacrament of Holy Communion and is itself a sign of God's grace (a sacrament) for others;

- reproducing - to every disciple the commission is given to go and make disciples;

- a model of the kingdom - through acts of service, mercy, justice and compassion;

- a growing thing - Jesus gave the first disciples things to do which were highly formational;

- the key to resourcing new forms of church - generous giving of self, time and money are hallmarks of true discipleship;

- the spiritual soil in which Christian leaders grow - if fresh expressions of church are to proliferate then a whole host of new 'home-grown' leaders need to emerge.

For all of these reasons and more, discipleship matters. So how can we encourage the formation of new learners and followers of Jesus (learner and follower being the root meanings of the word disciple).

How was it for you?   10min 🏃

Invite people to discuss in twos the questions on the slide:

- How did the journey begin for you?
- What has helped you to grow as a disciple of Jesus?

Developing discipleship in fresh expressions 30min(20min) 💬

1. Supportive relationships

The Cable Street/Zac's Place story (choose which depending on which you featured earlier) highlights the importance of supportive relationships for the healthy development of disciples. A variety of different relationships are vital for discipleship - from one-to-one support, to small groups, to gatherings of the fresh expression, to joint ventures between local churches, to large nationwide celebrations. One-to-one support takes seriously Jesus' promise, 'Where two or three come together in my name, there I am with them' (Matthew 18.20). It can take at least two forms:

- companions are those who walk alongside each other as equals. They watch over one another in love, pray for one another, hold each other accountable and support, challenge and spur each other on.

- mentors and apprentices follow the example of Paul and Timothy. Paul mentored his apprentice Timothy, who was then encouraged to mentor others. Many labels are used of this process today - spiritual directors, soul friends, spiritual counsellors etc.

Small groups are crucial and the key learning community in many (if not most) fresh expressions - as they are (and have been) in most healthy churches throughout church history and around the world today. We see them in Acts, the Wesleyan revival, base ecclesial communities in Latin America and home churches at the heart of the prodigious growth of Christianity in China, to name just a few! They provide safe environments for individuals:

- to ask questions;

- to discuss aspects of the faith;

- to get to know a limited number of people well and develop a sense of belonging;

- to provide prayer and pastoral support for each other as people exercise their discipleship and share in mission wherever God has placed them in their day-to-day lives;
- to learn how to share their gifts and minister to one another.

2. Teaching and learning

In the great commission, Jesus is unequivocal about the need to teach disciples. The Greek word for disciple, 'mathetes', means 'one who learns'. Disciples are called to learn as they follow and churches have a responsibility to provide teaching in a way that helps disciples to learn.

As fresh expressions develop, three broad approaches to teaching and learning are emerging. The first, still fruitful, approach utilises published discipleship resources such as Disciples, Emmaus, Foundations21, Lifeshapes or Unlock (which is particularly helpful for those who struggle with literacy).

Other fresh expressions are developing their own courses and resources. This has the advantage of being developed in the midst of the culture and context in which the fresh expression is set. When developing materials 'in house' it is important to ask critical questions such as

- is it biblical?

- is it true to the Christian tradition?
- is it whole-life?
- is it both open and challenging?

The third approach sees many fresh expressions rediscovering ancient pathways of discipleship. The saints of today are being encouraged by revered saints of the past such as Brendan, Ignatius, Francis and Benedict. This new monastic approach uses daily biblical readings, rhythms and liturgies, spiritual exercises, contemplation, symbol and pilgrimage to deepen personal and corporate discipleship.

So how can you develop opportunities for discipleship within a fresh expression of church? Unlike many more traditional church plants, a fresh expression needs to think carefully about starting with a worship service. If you launch a service, you know who is probably going to come - Christians! So if the aim is to serve people who don't come to church, you may not get very far. Instead, as we have been saying, a fresh expression will come from listening to and following God's call (advance slide by one click).

Instead of starting with a worship service, fresh expressions are more likely to begin with loving service - a community café, a bus with food and videos for teenagers, an after-school club, a zone in which to relax and explore spirituality, a course on money management, a local campaign on behalf of asylum seekers... the possibilities are endless! (advance).

From the basis of loving service a community is formed (advance), faith is shared and explored - or to put it another way, evangelism and discipleship take place (advance) and church begins to take shape (advance). Part of this taking shape will include the emergence of contextually authentic forms of worship. This diagram is a summary of an initial process. In real life, the journey will be less linear and needs to become circular, as to stay fresh the newly forming church needs to keep doing all of the stages again (advance).

Building an experience of community within the context of loving service is vital. People may not come back if they don't feel accepted and valued. But if friendships form, the coffee may be dreadful (although it shouldn't be!), the talk can be really boring, the building may be down at heel but people will still turn up. They will come because they like each other. Creating community may be the biggest service you offer. But you will want to think about how you bring evangelism and discipleship into that community without changing its essence.

Some ideas

Here are three ways in which a fresh expression of church might encourage people to explore the way of Christian discipleship:

Include an explicitly Christian dimension from an early stage.

A luncheon club might put candles on the tables after the plates have been cleared, play some Christian music, read a few verses from Scripture, allow time for silent prayer and ask someone to read a couple of written prayers - all lasting about twenty minutes. Guests could leave after lunch if they wished, or stay on for this time of reflection. As prayers were answered, this short act of worship might lead to fortnightly Bible study after lunch, or a separate discipleship course.

Include a more general spiritual dimension from an early stage.

At the end of the evening, members of a divorce recovery group might be invited to share a period of quietness, in which they could pray or think positive thoughts about each other. The leader would quietly pray that the Holy Spirit graciously responds. In time, they might be invited to share with their neighbour their hopes and concerns about the coming week, and then pray for - or have positive thoughts about - the other person. Feedback on whether this was helpful might create openings for the group to discuss what God is like and how God gets involved in people's lives.

Create opportunities to form a separate discipleship group.

As relationships develop and personal evangelism takes place, some people may become interested in exploring the Christian faith. A group might meet at a different time of the week for this purpose. They may agree to do the Alpha course together or an equivalent.

As people explore Christianity together, they are not encouraged to join 'the main church', as has traditionally happened. They are invited to explore

This ideas section is optional and could be deleted if you are short of time. Continue from the group work which follows.

what it means to be church themselves as they meet, relate and begin to worship together. Mature church begins to develop when there is growth in all four key relationships of church - the upward or 'God-wards' (expressed in worship), the inward (fellowship), the outward (mission and evangelism) and the connected (catholicity - connection with the rest of the church).

Group work

Use your prepared rucksack to illustrate the following explanation.

Now it's time to grab a drink and take a look at this 'rucksack for discipleship' I prepared earlier. Think how you would prepare a group of people new to the Christian faith for the journey of discipleship? Consider:

- Who would be part of the journey? Don't forget Jesus! Note how those exploring faith can sharpen faith in others - healthy discipleship communities are places of mutual learning, not groups of experts and empty vessels. Jesus used the questions and comments of others to allow truth to emerge in the midst of conversation.

- What resources or tools would take to guide and equip you?

- What food would sustain you on the journey?

- How would you travel? What rhythms might you follow, where and when might you meet to communicate, what significant markers might you look for on the journey?

- What would you do?

Encourage/enable the groups to generate the ideas on sheets of flipchart paper. You may wish to bring to the session your own checklist of components (that you feel are important) to affirm what the groups produce and cover any gaps.

Give people 20min in groups to plan their journeys; then take feedback.

Pause for prayer or praise   5min 💬

Invite people to be still for a few moments whilst you play a piece of reflective music. Ask people to think about their experience of being disciples and to let a silent prayer form out of that reflection. A good song to use would be *Covenant* [3.17], written by pioneering minister Jeff Reynolds and performed by his band *The Smiling Strangers* (**thesmilingstrangers.com**). The song is taken from the album Dangerous Times, published by Maori Music and distributed by Confidential Records UK. It conveys powerfully the commitment that is at the heart of true Christian discipleship. You may find the song helpful for your own further reflections.

Alternatively, choose a suitable prayerful worship song (add to PowerPoint).

Section four: leadership - the journey continues

Introductory comments and DVD   10min 💬

We are now going to explore some issues relating to Christian leadership today. Before we open this up we need to note three key things:

1. Christian discipleship is foundational for Christian leadership. Before we are leaders, we are followers. If we are to have integrity in Christian leadership it is essential to be known as those who follow Christ. As leaders we are seeking to help others follow Jesus, not us.

2. Leaders come in all shapes and sizes and all Christians have their part to play in Christian leadership either directly, whether it be leading a home group, Messy Church session or a major denomination, or by encouraging and supporting others in their leadership. There is no stereotypical leader. It is not about 'alpha females or males'. Remember King David? He was hardly the obvious candidate to lead God's people but he was the one God chose.

3. Christian leadership is not confined to the Church! For the kingdom to come, Christian leaders in education, business, politics, the arts, the media and any other sector of life you can think of are essential! Whilst this unit will focus on leadership roles in fresh expressions of church, this is not meant to undervalue the Christian leadership exercised elsewhere.

These are interesting times for Christian leadership in the church. In many countries (especially the UK) and denominations there are far fewer ordained leaders active in Christian mission. At the same time in many countries, denominations and fresh expressions of church, a whole new wave of mission-shaped lay [not ordained] leaders is emerging. The future of ministry in fresh expressions will be mainly lay.

Case study

To illustrate how new leaders are emerging in fresh expressions, show one of:

* re:generation [6.36];
* St George's [6.53] (delete the re:generation image on the slide to reveal the St George's 'beach' image).

Leadership in a fresh expression of church   30min (20min)

The features of leadership listed here are reproduced on the handout for this unit.

There is nothing new in God raising up leaders in mission for the Christian church. For the longer *mission shaped ministry* course, Joanne Cox identified 13 characteristics from the ministries of Paul and Barnabas that are highly relevant for those seeking to grow new forms of church and make new disciples today. Leadership is about:

* noticing and discerning potential and putting your own reputation on the line when appropriate - it is about being a person of recognisable character (Acts 9.23-30);
* spending time mentoring other people - this can take a long time (Acts 11.25-30);
* being chosen, commissioned and prayerfully set aside for a task by a bigger group of people (Acts 12.25-13.3);
* stepping up at the opportune moment and letting the succession continue - and stepping back at the opportune moment (Acts 13.4-12);
* using your experience and background as well as knowing the context to which you are speaking (Acts 13.16-45);
* accepting persecution - the challenge is to stay on track (Acts 13.46-52);

- knowing when to leave and when to stay (Acts 14.1-7);
- pointing to someone greater (Acts 14.8-18);
- being ready to get hurt - it is not always a bed of roses but you need to know that there are other people who will gather around and walk back to the 'city' with you (Acts 14.19-20);
- being accountable and testifying honestly to what God is doing (Acts 14.26-28);
- asking tough theological questions and wrestling with the answers in the midst of those wiser and more discerning (Acts 15.1-21);
- discerning the right team at the right time (Acts 15.22-35);
- being ready for conflict - succession is a mark of success (Acts 15.36-41).

Here are some further reflections on the qualities that leaders of fresh expressions of church will need.

Willingness to take risks

Fresh expressions are uncharted territory. A common cry of pioneers in fresh expressions is this... 'We don't really know what we are doing'. It will be important to rest on your sense of calling and seek confidence in God in this.

There will be exposure to scrutiny. At least in the early stages you will stand out and be scrutinised by local churches, leaders, members, local community and media. This is quite correct and we should expect to give an account for what we are establishing. Any form of church leadership is a public role in the wider community.

There will be a high risk of failure. This is true in all leadership but when leading people into uncertainty, precarious positions and untried forms of community and worship, failure is more likely.

As a leader, you will need to be able to cope with this. Some comments may be unfairly negative and critical. Yes, learn humility, be open-minded, be a listener and weigh people's comments about what you are doing but don't let people talk you out of a radical idea if you are confident in it - it might simply be that they just can't see it. It doesn't mean that your ideas are wrong. Be unreasonable if necessary!

Fresh expressions provide multiple challenges to our basic assumptions, pre-conceptions, traditions and theologies.

A leader of a fresh expression initiative went to speak to members of local churches about her church. She was told that her initiative was 'dangerous'.

True or not, would this be a bad thing? Was Jesus a 'dangerous' leader?

Leadership for this time of change, as we navigate this seascape, will necessarily involve risk and that risk may well come at a price.

Leading together

There are only two references to solitary leadership in the New Testament. All of the other references are communal. Gone are the days when the church leader was the expert who told others what to think and who did most of the work, carrying the burden of the church. The Bible is full of surprising choices for leadership roles - Peter, an impetuous fisherman who often made mistakes, went on to be a leader in the early church.

The leaders who will thrive in fresh expressions are those who are able to see the potential in others and who give them space to develop their gifts. This should lead us to embrace 'us' - the variety of Christians in community, to value what each brings, and the multi-faceted nature of the Christian community.

Leadership for this time of change, navigating this seascape, will be leadership which is shared, and values team.

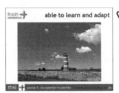

Able to learn and adapt

It could be said that the learners shall inherit the earth. Effective leaders are learners (disciples) first and then teachers.

Because society is fluid and constantly changing, and because there is not just one culture but many that overlap and are interconnected, we will have to be quick learners and supremely adaptable. Some will be called to lead or to help Christian communities to navigate this ever-changing 'seascape'. We can try hard to work out exactly what form of church is appropriate in our neighbourhood, culture and time, and then set that up. But we will still have the challenge that we must remain open to doing the same exercise a few years later when the context for mission will certainly have changed.

Creativity and imagination are increasingly important gifts for leadership. It was Einstein who said 'you will never see what you cannot imagine'.

Film clip

We're going to watch a clip from *The Wrong Trousers*. Wallace and Gromit have taken in a lodger; a mysterious penguin who hijacks Wallace's Techno Trousers and uses them in a robbery. He's about to make off with the diamond that he stole when Gromit confronts him with a rolling pin.

The clip starts at the beginning of chapter 6 as Wallace confronts the penguin with a rolling pin (0:23:24). It ends after Wallace says 'Well done! We did it!' (0:26:22).

People who have started a fresh expression often talk of the way ahead becoming clear as they moved forward i.e. the track being laid as they were moving along. God led them into new ways of being church together, and they needed to be able to think on their feet and adapt to their environment and the people they met.

Exercise

In your groups, please choose one of the scenarios on the slide and produce a team leadership specification.

What sort of leaders would you need for your chosen scenario? Describe their roles and the gifts and character you would be looking for:

1. You are a team planting a fresh expression of church in one of the following:

   - a residential home for elderly people;

   - an academy or high school;

   - a village hall;

   - a Messy Church;

   - a scenario of your own choice appropriate to your own context.

2. You are a church excited by what you have learnt on *msi* and are looking to become more mission-shaped.

Section five: closing meditation

Spiral galaxy meditation

10min

This works best in the centre of the room on a space cleared before the session. It would be good to darken the room, except for the screen and a spotlight on the floor. Place thin, white material, such as inexpensive muslin or calico on the floor to make an area about three metres square ready for the activity. Place a few stars or counters on the material. Play some meditative music during this activity.

Let the first pattern of stars represent people in a community with each star representing a person. Lonely, beautiful lights, unique. Look at the stars; let them remind you of your own local community and networks.

We have been thinking about the journey towards Christ that each of us is on. A church contains people, disciples, all on that same journey, each of them starting from different places and going at a different pace. But the church needs to be a naturally attractive community as if it had a gravity of its own, drawing people towards Jesus Christ, its centre, without it necessarily having a clear edge or boundary.

Pause - leave time for people to engage with the image.

So picture now a cluster galaxy - the stars being drawn in toward its centre. Some stars are very close to the centre, others remain far away. There is no clear edge or boundary - every star is influenced by this gravity, some more than others.

Pause.

Now enjoy the fully developed system, this beautiful image of a galaxy with its spiral arms sweeping out into the stars around as if gathering in stars as it spins. We could imagine a Christ centred community in this image, gathering in people by Godly gravity!

Invite the group to create a spiral galaxy on the floor.

Take some of the stars or counters. Chose a number of them to represent people you know - Christians or others. You may wish to think of those you know in Christian leadership within or beyond the church. Bring them into the centre and place them on the material in a place that corresponds to that person's relationship with God - close to the centre, on the outskirts or further away.

As you place your star, pray for God to draw that person closer to himself, that they would remain or become true disciples.

Close in prayer. You might like to use this prayer written by Ian Adams for msi, based on Philippians 2.15, which links to the spiral galaxy meditation.

Holy trinity, you are at work in us and in this world.
Sometimes called to be leaders, always called to be disciples.
Help us to live without murmuring or arguing.
Help us to be blameless and innocent.
Help us to shine like stars. Amen.

Finish

Thank people for coming, point out the book recommendations on the handout and confirm the arrangements for the next session.

Recommended resources

 Recommended resources

- **Disciples and Citizens: A Vision for Distinctive Living**
Graham Cray, IVP, 2007, 978-1844741517-1.

- **Finding Our Way Again: The Return of the Ancient Practices**
Brian McLaren, Thomas Nelson Publishers, 2008, 978-084994602-8.

- **The Call and the Commission: Equipping a New Generation of Leaders for a New World**
Rob Frost, David Wilkinson and Joanne Cox (eds.), Paternoster, 2009, 978-1842276082.

- **Growing Leaders: Reflections on Leadership, Life and Jesus**
James Lawrence, BRF, 2004, 978-1841012469.

- <u>deepeningdiscipleship.org.uk</u>.

 God grows church through reproduction
<u>freshexpressions.org.uk/guide/about/principles/reproduction</u>

God wants people to become disciples of Jesus
<u>freshexpressions.org.uk/guide/about/principles/disciples</u>

6. where do we go from here?

Introduction

Aim

To provide space for people to consider their response to this course and what they might do next.

Outline and timings

These notes are written as a script which you can use 'as is' or adapt to your own needs and experiences. Text in this type is notes for the leader, not to be read out.

The material is designed for a two hour session with the times given in the 120min column to the right. To reduce to a 90 minute session we suggest using the timings in the 90min column, or adapting the material yourself to suit the emphasis of your group.

Where do we go from here?		120min	90min
Section one: welcome, introductions and worship		**10min**	**5min**
Welcome	💬	2min	2min
Worship and prayer	🐑	8min	3min
Section two: from listening to action		**65min**	**55min**
Listening - a key skill	💬+🎨+🎨+👥	25min	20min
Daring to dream	👥	30min	25min
Pause for praise and prayer	🐑	10min	10min
Section three: my response		**25min**	**20min**
What journey have you been on?	🐑	10min	10min
Next steps	💬+👥	15min	10min
Section four: commissioning		**20min**	**10min**
Commissioning	🐑	20min	10min

Session checklist

Media

Equipment to show clips - laptop, projector, DVD player, TV as required.

A clip from the week's news, if required.

The Color Purple clip (Spielberg, 1985).

From the course DVD:
* Listening for mission [4.57]
  chapter 6 from *expressions: the dvd - 2*

Instrumental reflective music and means of playing it, for the journey section.

Any song words required.

Other materials

Prayer tree and cards.

Paper and pens.

Art materials for daring to dream exercise.

For the commissioning:
* a small bowl of tea-lights on each table, a large candle and matches;
* one or two small bottles of scented oil.

Feedback forms for participants (photocopied from p126 or downloaded and printed from the course website).

Section one: welcome, introductions and worship

Welcome   2min 💬

Welcome participants and give a quick recap of the material so far in the course:

- In our first session we considered the *Mission-shaped Church* report and its impact;

- In the second session we looked at our changing world and the way the church needs to respond;

- In the third session we explored the need for authentic community within church in a consumerist society;

- In the fourth session we discussed the need to re-imagine worship;

- In the fifth session we looked at the need to deepen discipleship and encourage new leadership.

- In this session we will be asking where we go from here.

Worship and prayer   8min (3min) 🗣️

Choose a worship song to sing together and add the words to the PowerPoint. After the song, pray for God's blessing on the session. If appropriate, you could ask one or two people in the group to pray.

As an alternative, to keep people mindful of the needs of the world that so often form the context for mission, you could show a video clip from the local TV news of the day or week, choosing an item that demonstrates the concerns of people right now in your locality. Ask people to tell their neighbour what their instinctive reaction is to this issue (positive or negative). Then suggest that all of our responses and reactions can be brought to God who has compassion for us, for our locality and for the wider world - and choose a song to sing together that reflects this.

Section two: from listening to action

Listening - a key skill   25min (20min)

In this session we're looking at what happens next. So far we have shown:

*   how the mission belongs to God and is shaped by God's character;
*   that it is God who invites us to join in;
*   that the church is the fruit of mission and not vice versa;
*   how these are exciting times in the life of the church and many people from pioneers of fresh expressions to senior leaders of denominations are encouraging Godly risks and adventures in mission - there is permission to dream;
*   that for the new to emerge, sometimes we have to stop things.

So how might you take all that we've covered over the last five sessions and act on it in your local area? Where do you begin? Before we dive straight in we need to listen and check what we are hearing.

The Color Purple

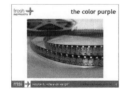

We're going to watch a clip from the film *The Color Purple*. It tells the life story of Celie, a woman growing up in the US at the beginning of the 20th century, who has an incredibly hard life. This clip comes towards the end of the film. The local community is roughly split in two with the righteous going to church and the rest gathering at Harpo's speakeasy out in the woods. Shug Avery is a singer who has had a long-term affair with Celie's husband, but the two are now friends. Shug's father is the pastor of the local church, but they are estranged as he doesn't approve of her lifestyle. In this clip, Shug is singing at the speakeasy while the faithful gather at church.

 Start at chapter 37 (02:12:19), end after the reconciliation as 'Maybe God is trying to tell you something' is sung (02:16:55).

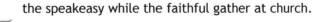

Both parts of the community sing to each other 'Maybe God is trying to tell you something'. We feel we have a message for the rest of the world: people need to listen to God's call on their life. The reality is that God is also trying to speak to us through the culture around us and the people who are outside the church but in whose lives God is already working. So as we respond to the issues we have covered over these sessions, the key skill we need is the ability to listen. Maybe God is trying to tell us something!

Jesus was a great listener, and he started young. When he was twelve, Mary and Joseph took him to Jerusalem for the Passover feast. Afterwards, they set off for home thinking that he was with their group, but when they stopped for the night they discovered he wasn't there. They went back to Jerusalem and had a very anxious three days trying to find Jesus. Luke 2.46 tells us, 'After three days they found him in the temple, sitting among the teachers, listening to them and asking them questions.' Jesus felt at home in the temple; he called it his Father's house and yet was still ready to listen and to learn.

Jesus kept on asking questions throughout his ministry - to the man at the pool waiting to be healed (John 5.6); to the centurion whose servant was ill (Matthew 8.7); to the woman who touched him wanting to be healed (Luke 8.45) and to the disciples, asking them who they thought he was (Luke 9.18-20). Jesus listened to people and responded to their need rather than treating everyone in a uniform way.

We saw this diagram briefly last session.

As we think about developing fresh expressions of church, there are three vital strands that need to develop alongside each other.

1. prayer and support

    The prayers of the wider Christian community are essential.

2. connection

It is vital that fresh expressions remain connected to, committed to and accountable to the wider Body of Christ. And it is vital that the wider Body of Christ supports, resources and prays for the fresh expression.

3. listening to God

Discerning his call and following that call, through prayer, the Scriptures, other Christians and God's world.

Earlier in the course we thought about the bread-making community *Somewhere Else* in Liverpool, where Barbara Glasson was sent as a minister to the town centre with no church and no congregation. She ended up walking the streets for several months, listening to where people were at and what their needs were - and the community grew from that. She also listened carefully to God and was very surprised when one day, heading into Liverpool on the train, she heard God speak the word 'bread' into her mind. That moment of listening combined with the hours of patient listening on the streets has proved to be inspirational for many people in Liverpool and beyond as the story has been shared.

We need to listen with our ears, our minds, our hearts and our imaginations - we shall return to the latter shortly.

So how do we listen? This clip gives some advice from different people who are involved in fresh expressions of church.

Discussion

Show the listening for mission clip [4.57]. After the clip, invite people to respond to what was said. Which comment would fit their situation? How have they been listening to their own communities? What has worked for them? Spend about 10 minutes on this.

Daring to dream

30min (25min)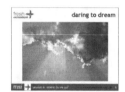

It is time to do a little dreaming. Imagine a culture or context or group of people amongst whom you long to see God's love being made known. Now imagine what form of fresh expression might serve these people, form community with them, explore faith and encourage discipleship amongst them and allow a new form of church to emerge with culturally authentic worship and mission at its heart. What does it look like? Who is part of it? Where and when is it meeting? What is going on?

Dare to dream! Don't let the sceptics and naysayers hold sway. For the next 25 minutes the following phrases are banned: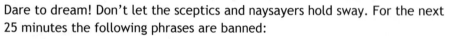

*   it will never work;

*   we couldn't do that;

*   we've tried that before.

Let your heart beat a little faster, be excited by what God could do and remember the words of the angel to Mary, 'nothing is impossible with God' (Luke 1.37).

Grab a drink and then, in twos or small groups, sketch out your dream in words or pictures. Art materials are available if you would like to use these.

Pause for praise and prayer

10min

Invite people to draw a picture of their dream on a piece of card and place it on the prayer tree that you have prepared. Then either offer a prayer over the dreams yourself or invite members of the group to pray for the dreams that have been shared.

You may also wish to choose a suitable worship song and add the words to the PowerPoint.

♪ **Be thou my vision** Various versions *Song*

Section three: my response

What journey have you been on? 10min

Invite people to spend some time on their own thinking about the journey they have been on in the last few sessions. Invite them to take paper and pens and to write down their current thinking. They may want to call it 'The view from here'.

Some people may have experienced a change in their thinking, arriving at a better understanding of what fresh expressions of church are all about. Others may be feeling a more specific call to explore further what a fresh expression of church might look like for their particular community, or even to set one up. Still others may be called to help their present church to be more missional. Explain that you will offer suggestions for next steps in the penultimate part of this unit.

There is no uniform outcome to this course: God may be saying different things to different people. Encourage people to feed into this reflection anything that came out of the dreaming exercise earlier.

You may wish to play reflective music quietly in the background. After about seven or eight minutes, invite people to pray in twos and threes for each other.

Next steps

15min (10min) 💬 👥

On your handout are details of further resources from Fresh Expressions that you may find helpful as you continue on this journey:

* DVDs, booklets and books available from freshexpressions.org.uk/shop;
* two resources to help you share what you have learnt with others - *vision days* (freshexpressions.org.uk/vision) and *mission shaped congregations*, a CD-ROM with service or small group material (freshexpressions.org.uk/resources/congregations);
* *mission shaped ministry*, the sister course to this one for those who feel called to pursue their dreams. We strongly recommend *mission shaped ministry*, which explores in much more depth the joys and challenges of developing new forms of church (freshexpressions.org.uk/missionshapedministry);
* the website freshexpressions.org.uk;
* The Guide freshexpressions.org.uk/guide, an online guide to fresh expressions of church.
* *e-xpressions*, the free monthly email bulletin freshexpressions.org.uk/signup.

Does anyone have any questions or comments about any aspect of the course? This is your final chance to interact with this group on these issues!

Encourage people to ask questions about the course and to feedback on their experiences of it. You may wish to ask participants to complete feedback forms at this point, or after the session finishes.

The workbook contains additional resources to those listed above.

Section four: commissioning

Commissioning   20min (10min) 🗪

We have come a long way over these six sessions of *msi* and our prayer is that God's Spirit would hover over all that has been heard, seen and spoken and bring new things to birth. We place our trust in God and we answer to God, because ultimately it is God's mission we are involved in. God is already going before us, preparing works for us to do.

Mission is seeing what God is doing and joining in. But the place to end is the place at which the psalmists begin. Whatever our strategies or dreams, they're lifeless without the Spirit. The church is infinitely precious to God. God is totally passionate about his people - and God has no other plan.

It is to God alone that we entrust our future and God's power alone can enable us to move forward in such a way that society around us is blessed and renewed.

So let's bring all our whirring thoughts to the foot of the cross, as we pray together.

Lord, we are honoured that you call us your friends.
Call us afresh to know and experience your love;
For you love us and want to enjoy us forever.
Fill us afresh with your Holy Spirit that we may use the gifts you have given each one of us with courage and compassion;
For you love us and want to enjoy us forever.

Open our eyes Lord, to see your grace at work beyond our church buildings and institutions;
For you love us and want to enjoy us forever.
Help us Lord, to work with you in building communities of faith allowing your mission to be expressed in our hurting world;
For you love us and want to enjoy us forever.

6. where do we go from here?

May we proclaim afresh your faithfulness and constant love in a changing and uncertain world;
For you love us and want to enjoy us forever.
Let us see with the eyes of faith;
For mission is seeing what God is doing and joining in.
For the building of your kingdom and to the glory of your name;
Through Jesus Christ our Lord. Amen.

I light this candle to symbolise Jesus, the light of the world.

Light the large candle at the front.

In a moment I would like to invite you to take a tea-light candle from the plate on your table and as a symbolic response to come and form a cross of light here on this table - lighting your light from the large candle.

Then if you would like to, you can be anointed with oil and prayed for, that God would fill you afresh with his Spirit and equip you with all you need to follow God's calling.

In this act we are offering ourselves afresh for God's service, for his mission wherever he has called you and to whomever he has called you.

God may be calling you to prepare to begin a new work.
He may be calling you to revisit something that you already are doing but to re-work it.
Unbelievable as it may seem - you are a part of God's plan.

♪ Tim Hughes
Light of the world *Song*
Thankyou Music, 2000

Taizé Community
The Lord is my light
Taizé Community, 1984

John Bell, Graham Maule
Jesus Christ is waiting
Iona Community, 1988

Sing together as people light their candles, placing them in the shape of the cross. You will need to add the words to the PowerPoint. Have one or two people standing to one side with small bottles of scented oil. They should put oil on their finger and then mark the shape of the cross on people's foreheads as they pray for them to be anointed with God's Spirit and equipped for the task ahead.

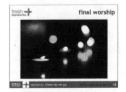

Then invite people to join in this final prayer of blessing together

May the fire of Christ consume all indifference to God,
The light of Christ illumine our vision of God,
The love of Christ enlarge our longing for God,
The Spirit of Christ empower our service to God,
And the blessing of God Almighty
The Father, the Son and the Holy Spirit
Be among us, and remain with us always, Amen.

Finish

Thank people for coming and remind them of the information on the handout. Don't forget feedback forms.

Is God calling me to be involved?
freshexpressions.org.uk/guide/about/god

web

Thank you!

Thank you for teaching *mission shaped intro* - we hope you found it inspiring and helpful. If you have suggestions or comments please do get in touch with us at
msi@freshexpressions.org.uk.

Don't forget to collate course participants' evaluations and send them to us at missionshapedministry.org/evaluate.

Resources and photocopy sheets

Recommended reading

Books

- **Mission-shaped Church (second edition)**
  Graham Cray, CHP, 2004, 978-071514189-2.

- **Fresh! An introduction to fresh expressions of church and pioneer ministry**
  David Goodhew, Andrew Roberts, Michael Volland, SCM, 2012, 978-033404387-4.

- **Church for every context: An introduction to theology and practice**
  Michael Moynagh, SCM Press, 2012, 978-033404369-0

- **changing church for a changing world**
  Pete Pillinger, Andrew Roberts, MPH, 2007, 978-185852335-4.

- **Pioneers 4 Life**
  David Male (ed.), BRF, 2011, 978-184101827-0.

- **Resourcing Renewal: Shaping Churches for the Emerging Future**
  Martyn Atkins, Inspire, 2007, 978-190595810-8.

- **God-Shaped Mission: Theological and Practical Perspectives from the Rural Church**
  Alan Smith, Canterbury Press Norwich, 2008, 978-185311807-4.

DVDs

- **expressions: making a difference**
  Norman Ivison, Fresh Expressions, 2011, 978-0-9560005-4-5.

- **Sanctus: fresh expressions of church in the sacramental tradition**
  Norman Ivison, Fresh Expressions, 2009, 978-0-9560005-3-8.

- **expressions: the dvd - 2: changing church in every place**
  Norman Ivison, CHP, 2007, 978-071514128-1.

- **expressions: the dvd - 1: stories of church for a changing culture**
  Norman Ivison, CHP, 2006, 978-071514095-6.

Fresh Expressions
freshexpressions.org.uk

web

The Guide, exploring fresh expressions of church together
freshexpressions.org.uk/guide

Fresh Expressions online shop, where you can purchase all resources on this page except those marked *
freshexpressions.org.uk/shop

Share booklets

- **How can fresh expressions emerge? (Share booklet 01)**
  Michael Moynagh with Andy Freeman, Fresh Expressions, 2011, 978-0-9568123-1-5.

- **How should we start? (Share booklet 02)**
  Michael Moynagh with..., Fresh Expressions, 2011, 978-0-9568123-2-2.

- **What should we start? (Share booklet 03)**
  Michael Moynagh with..., Fresh Expressions, 2011, 978-0-9568123-3-9.

- **How can we get support? (Share booklet 04)**
  Michael Moynagh with..., Fresh Expressions, 2011, 978-0-9568123-4-6.

- **How can we find our way? (Share booklet 05)**
  Michael Moynagh with..., Fresh Expressions, 2011, 978-0-9568123-5-3.

- **How can we be sustainable? (Share booklet 06)**
  Michael Moynagh with..., Fresh Expressions, 2011, 978-0-9568123-6-0.

- **How can we be a great team? (Share booklet 07)**
  Michael Moynagh with..., Fresh Expressions, 2011, 978-0-9568123-7-7.

- **How can we finance a fresh expression? (Share booklet 08)**
  John Preston, Andrew Roberts, Fresh Expressions, 2012, 978-095681238-4.

- **How can we encourage a fresh expression? (Share booklet 09)**
  Michael Moynagh, Fresh Expressions, 2012, 978-095681239-1.

- **How should we teach and preach? (Share booklet 10)**
  Norman Ivison, Fresh Expressions, 2013, 978-095756840-2.

Further titles are released regularly, visit the Share booklets page at freshexpressions.org.uk/share/booklets for the latest information.

Feedback and evaluation form

An important process for us is the evaluation of this course by participants, which helps the ongoing development of this and future courses. We would be grateful for your honest and critical feedback.

Please rate your response to each question from 0 (very negative) to 10 (very positive).

1. Did the course content meet your expectations from the pre-course information?

   0   1   2   3   4   5   6   7   8   9   10

2. Was the course material interesting, fun and informative?

   0   1   2   3   4   5   6   7   8   9   10

3. Was there enough opportunity for interaction with (A) presenters (B) participants?

   (A) 0   1   2   3   4   5   6   7   8   9   10
   (B) 0   1   2   3   4   5   6   7   8   9   10

4. Please rate each week's session on its content and delivery:

   (1) 0   1   2   3   4   5   6   7   8   9   10
   (2) 0   1   2   3   4   5   6   7   8   9   10
   (3) 0   1   2   3   4   5   6   7   8   9   10
   (4) 0   1   2   3   4   5   6   7   8   9   10
   (5) 0   1   2   3   4   5   6   7   8   9   10
   (6) 0   1   2   3   4   5   6   7   8   9   10

5. Do you have any comments on the learning layout used (ie. café-style)?

6. Any other comments?

Please return the form to your course organiser. You do not need to put your name on it. Thank you!

Appendix 1: relationships (session 3, p59)

Photocopy this page and cut out each Bible verse. This exercise is adapted from Phil Potter, *The Challenge of Cell Church*, BRF, 2001.

Love one another with mutual affection; outdo one another in showing honour (Romans 12.10)

Be kind to one another, tender-hearted, forgiving one another as God in Christ has forgiven you (Ephesians 4.32)

Exhort one another every day (Hebrews 3.13)

Provoke one another to love and good deeds (Hebrews 10.24)

Confess your sins to one another, and pray for one another, so that you may be healed (James 5.16)

Bear one another's burdens (Galatians 6.2)

Welcome one another (Romans 15.7)

Be subject to one another out of reverence for Christ (Ephesians 5.21)

Through love become slaves to one another (Galatians 5.13)

Bear with one another (Colossians 3.13)

Appendix 2: sheets for creative worship exercise (session 4, p84)

Photocopy these two pages onto two sheets of A4 and cut out each rectangle. There are two each of five seasons, two each of five senses and one each of ten objects.

Advent	Advent	Christmas	Christmas
Easter	Easter	Lent	Lent
Pentecost	Pentecost	taste	taste
touch	touch	smell	smell

hearing	hearing	sight	sight
play dough	feather	stone	chocolate
candle	grapes	paper	balloon
Ice cube	map of local area	clothing	piece of string

Published 2013 by Fresh Expressions
Registered charity #1080103

Copyright © Fresh Expressions 2013
freshexpressions.org.uk

Fresh Expressions, The Benn Centre,
Claremont Road, Rugby, CV21 3LU
0300 365 0563

Author: Fresh Expressions
Contributors: See full credits to the right
Designer: Ben Clymo

freshexpressions.org.uk/
missionshapedintro

ISBN 978-0-9560005-5-2

fresh expressions

Credits

This course was first devised and run by Tony Hardy of CPAS and Sally Thornton. Further revision and editing by Ian Adams, Tim Atkins, Jenny Baker, Kelly Betteridge, Karen Carter, Ben Clymo, Ross Garner, Wayne Hawkins, Bev Hollings, Norman Ivison, Rachel Jordan, Phil Joyce, Tim Lea, Stephen Lindridge, Bruce and Colleen Mounsey, Sheonagh Ormrod, Ruth Poch, Linda Rayner, Jeff Reynolds, Andrew Roberts, Abigail Rose, Pam Smith, Martyn Snow, Sally Thornton and Tim Woolley.

Partners

Thanks to our *msi* partners: Church Army, Church of England, CMS, Congregational Federation, CWM Europe, Ground Level Network, Methodist Church, United Reformed Church.

Course workbook

Course workbooks for participants (ISBN 978-09560005-6-9) are available to purchase from our online shop: freshexpressions.org.uk/shop.